Lab Manual

Chemistry

Shoreview, Minnesota

Pearson AGS Globe™ is a trademark of Pearson Education, Inc.
Pearson® is a registered trademark of Pearson plc.

ISBN 0-7854-4053-4

A 0 9 8 7 6 5 4 3 2 1

1-800-328-2560
www.agsglobe.com

Table of Contents

Table of Contents, continued

Table of Contents, continued

Safety Rules and Symbols

In this book, you will learn about chemistry through investigations and labs. During these activities, it is important to follow safety rules, procedures, and your teacher's directions. You can avoid accidents by following directions and handling materials carefully. Read and follow the safety rules below, and learn the safety symbols. To alert you to possible dangers, safety symbols will appear with each investigation or lab. Reread the rules below often and review what the symbols mean.

General Safety

◆ Read each Express Lab, Investigation, and Discovery Investigation before doing it. Review the materials list and follow the safety symbols and safety alerts.

◆ Ask questions if you do not understand something.

◆ Never perform an experiment, mix substances, or use equipment without permission.

◆ Keep your work area clean and free of clutter.

◆ Be aware of other students working near you.

◆ Do not play or run during a lab activity. Take your lab work seriously.

◆ Know where fire extinguishers, fire alarms, first aid kits, fire blankets, and the nearest telephone are located. Be familiar with the emergency exits and evacuation route from your room.

◆ Keep your hands away from your face.

◆ Immediately report all accidents to your teacher, including injuries, broken equipment, and spills.

◆ Wash your hands when you are finished with a lab activity.

Eye Protection

◆ Wear safety goggles at all times or as directed by your teacher.

◆ If a substance gets in your eyes or on your face, use an eyewash station or flush youreyes and face with running water immediately. Tell your teacher.

Clothing Protection

◆ Wear a lab coat or apron at all times or as directed by your teacher.

◆ Tie back long hair, remove dangling jewelry, and secure loose-fitting clothing.

◆ Do not wear open-toed shoes, sandals, or canvas shoes in the lab.

Safety Rules and Symbols, continued

Hand Safety
◆ Wear protective gloves when directed by your teacher.
◆ Do not touch an object that could be hot.
◆ Use tongs or utensils to hold a container over a heat source.
◆ Wash your hands when you are finished with a lab activity.

Flame/Heat Safety
◆ Clear your work space of materials that could burn or melt.
◆ Before using a burner, know how to operate the burner and gas outlet.
◆ Be aware of all open flames. Never reach across a flame.
◆ Never leave a flame or operating hot plate unattended.
◆ Do not heat a liquid in a closed container.
◆ When heating a substance in a test tube or flask, point the container away from yourself and others.
◆ Do not touch hot glassware or the surface of an operating hot plate or lightbulb.
◆ In the event of a fire, tell your teacher and leave the room immediately.
◆ If your clothes catch on fire, stop, drop to the floor, and roll.

Chemical Safety
◆ Check labels on containers to be sure you are using the right substance.
◆ Do not directly smell any substance. If you are instructed to smell a substance, gently fan your hand over the substance, waving its vapors toward you.
◆ When handling substances that give off gases or vapors, work in a fume hood or well-ventilated area.
◆ Do not taste any substance. Never eat, drink, or chew gum in your work area.
◆ Do not return unused substances to their original containers.
◆ Avoid skin contact with substances used in lab. Some substances can irritate or harm skin.
◆ If a substance spills on your clothing or skin, rinse the area immediately with plenty of water. Tell your teacher.

Measurement and Precision

Use with Discovery Investigation 1, pages 24–25

Materials   safety goggles   water
          lab coat or apron   metric measuring cup
          small plastic bottle   100-mL graduated cylinder

Different measuring tools measure with different precision. The amount of precision is based on the measuring units marked on each tool. In this investigation, you will measure three volumes of water using two different tools. Which tool will measure with greater precision?

Procedure

1. To record your data, make a data table like the one shown here.

Amount of Water	Volume (mL)	
	Measuring Cup	**Graduated Cylinder**
full bottle		
half bottle		
quarter bottle		

2. Design an experiment to find out which measuring tool is more precise. You will measure three different volumes using each tool. For the first measurement, fill the bottle with water. For the second measurement, fill the bottle about half full. For the last measurement, fill it about one-fourth full.

3. Write a procedure for your experiment. Include a hypothesis and any Safety Alerts.

4. Have your hypothesis and procedure approved by your teacher.

5. Put on safety goggles and a lab coat or apron.

6. Carry out your experiment. Record your results. Make sure you record only significant figures (the certain digits and one uncertain digit).

Measurement and Precision, continued

Cleanup/Disposal

Clean your work area and return the materials.

Analysis

1. How precisely can you measure using the measuring cup?

_____

2. How precisely can you measure using the graduated cylinder?

_____

3. How do the two recorded values for each volume compare?

_____

Conclusions

1. Which measuring tool was more precise?

_____

2. How do you know which tool was more precise?

_____

Explore Further

Design a similar investigation to measure length. Use one ruler that
is marked in only centimeters and another ruler that is marked in
centimeters and millimeters.

Accurate Volume Measurements

Why do scientists use so many different pieces of lab equipment? One reason is scientists that require accurate measurements. Volume is one type of measurement. In this investigation, you will practice measuring volume using three pieces of glassware. In addition, you will learn to calculate percent error. Percent error is the measure of the accuracy of your answer compared to an accepted accurate value. The formula for percent error is:

$$\text{percent error} = \frac{\text{difference between measured value and accepted value}}{\text{accepted value}} \times 100\%$$

Finding your percent error is much like grading yourself. If you only have a 4% error, your work is 96% accurate!

Materials safety goggles
lab coat or apron
100-mL graduated cylinder
wash bottle containing distilled water

50-mL buret in stand
100-mL beaker
calculator

Procedure

1. Put on safety goggles and a lab coat or apron.

2. Fill the empty buret with distilled water until it is above the 0.00 mark (at the top). Release a small amount until the meniscus rests on the 0.00-mL line. This fills the air space at the bottom of the buret. **Safety Alert: Handle glass with care. Report any broken or chipped glass to your teacher immediately. Wipe up all spills immediately.**

3. Dispense exactly 25.00 mL of water from the buret into the graduated cylinder. Read and record the water volume in the cylinder. Record your observation about the certainty of this measurement. Find and record the difference between the buret and the graduated cylinder measurements.

Accurate Volume Measurements, continued

Glassware	Volume(mL)	Difference from 25.00 mL	Observations About Certainty of Measurement
buret			
graduated cylinder			
beaker			

4. Pour the contents of the graduated cylinder into the beaker. Does the beaker show exactly 25.00 mL? Record your observation about the certainty of this measurement. Find and record the difference between the graduated cylinder and beaker.

Cleanup/Disposal

Wash the glassware, and return all materials. Clean your work area, and wash your hands.

Analysis

1. Calculate the percent error for the beaker measurement. The accurate value is 25.00 mL.

_____

2. What common metric unit is used to measure volume in the chemistry lab? _____

3. Calculate the percent error for the graduated cylinder measurement. The accurate value is 25.00 mL _____

Conclusions

1. Why is the buret a more accurate tool than the graduated cylinder?

_____

2. Which piece of glassware is usually not used for accurate volume measurements? Explain your answer.

_____

Accurate Volume Measurements, continued

3. What would have happened to your volume readings if there was air space at the bottom of the buret?

_____

Explore Further

Look at the Express Labs and Investigations in Chapters 1–3 of your text. Count the number of times a graduated cylinder and a beaker are used. Compare how the two kinds of glassware are used.

Density of Water and Ethanol

Density is an important physical property of a substance. It can be calculated from the mass and volume of a sample. The more particles of matter in a cubic centimeter, the denser the substance. Can you use density to identify an unknown substance? In this investigation, you will find out.

Materials   safety goggles   2 250-mL beakers
                lab coat or apron   distilled water
                digital balance   calculator
                50-mL graduated cylinder   2 different colored pencils
                30 mL of ethanol

Procedure

1. Put on safety goggles and a lab coat or apron.

2. Check that your digital balance is set to read in grams. **Safety Alert: Digital balances are extremely accurate and sensitive measuring devices. Do not press on the pan. Avoid spilling on it.**

3. Place the graduated cylinder on the balance. Press the tare button. The display should read 0.00. The balance will ignore the mass of the graduated cylinder. Do not remove the cylinder. **Safety Alert: Handle glass with care. Report any broken or chipped glass to your teacher immediately. Wipe up all spills immediately.**

4. Pour about 30.0 mL of ethanol into the beaker. Use this to pour close to 5 mL of ethanol into the graduated cylinder on the balance. Record the exact volume of ethanol in the table below.

   If some of the ethanol spills on the balance, start over. **Safety Alert: Alcohols are very flammable and explosive. Avoid breathing the vapors. Check that no open flames or spark-emitting electrical devices are nearby.**

Density of Water and Ethanol, continued

Ethanol			Distilled Water		
Volume(mL)	Mass(g)	Density (g/mL)	Volume(mL)	Mass(g)	Density (g/mL)

5. Record the exact mass of this sample.

6. Add more ethanol to the graduated cylinder until it contains close to 10 mL. Record the total volume of ethanol in the graduated cylinder. Record its total mass.

7. Repeat step 6, recording the exact volume and mass of samples close to 15, 20, and finally 25 mL.

8. Empty the ethanol in the graduated cylinder and beaker into the proper waste container. Never pour substances back into the original container. Clean the cylinder and beaker thoroughly, rinse with distilled water, and dry.

9. Repeat steps 3 through 8 using water instead of ethanol.

Cleanup/Disposal

Wash the glassware, and return all materials. Clean your work area, and wash your hands.

Analysis

1. Use a calculator to find the density of each of the ethanol and water samples. To calculate the density, divide mass by volume. Record your density value in the table.

Density of Water and Ethanol, continued

2. Why does density have a derived unit?

_____

3. What is the average density of ethanol? _____

4. What is the average density of water? _____

5. Compare the density of the two substances. _____

6. Percent error is used to determine the accuracy of measurements when an accepted value is known. The formula for percent error is:

$$\text{percent error} = \frac{\text{difference between measured value and accepted value}}{\text{accepted value}} \times 100\%$$

Conclusions

Use the *Handbook of Physics and Chemistry* to find the accepted values for the densities of ethanol and water. Calculate your percent error for each.

Substance	Average Density from Measured Values	Accepted Density Value	Percent Error
ethanol			
water			

Explore Further

The accepted density of water is 1.000 g/cm³. Ethanol is less dense and would therefore float on top of water. Investigate the density of several objects by testing if they sink or float in water and isopropanol (isopropyl alcohol or "rubbing alcohol"). Make hypotheses about their density. Test an ice cube as one of the objects.

Express Lab 2

Use with Express Lab 2, page 54

Materials   safety goggles
lab coat or apron
4 test tubes and rack
4 cm of magnesium ribbon
chalk dust
20 mL of a 5% vinegar solution
10-mL graduated cylinder
water

Procedure

1. Put on safety goggles and a lab coat or apron.

2. Examine the chalk and the magnesium. Record their physical properties.

3. Place the magnesium ribbon in a test tube. Place half of the chalk dust in another test tube.

4. Add 10 mL of water to each tube.

5. Record your observations. Include any evidence of chemical or physical changes. Remove the magnesium ribbon.

6. Repeat step 3 with the other two test tubes, using the same piece of magnesium. Add 10 mL of vinegar to each tube.

7. Record your observations, including any evidence of chemical or physical changes. Feel the bottom of each tube after any change.

Analysis

1. What happened when water was added to the magnesium and the chalk?

_____

2. What evidence did you see that chemical reactions occurred?

_____

Making Borax Putty

Can you think of a substance that has properties of two states of matter at one time? In this investigation, you will make a substance that has some physical properties of both a liquid and a solid. Borax putty flows like a liquid, but shatters like a solid.

Materials   safety goggles   paper towels
                   lab coat or apron   self-sealing plastic bag
                   water   white glue
                   stirring stick or spoon   4% sodium borate (borax) solution
                   5-ounce paper or plastic cup   digital balance
                   50-mL graduated cylinder

Procedure

1. Put on safety goggles and a lab coat or apron.

2. Measure 25 mL of glue into the graduated cylinder. Add 20 mL of water to the same graduated cylinder and stir well. Pour the mixture into the cup. **Safety Alert: Borax putty is nontoxic; however, this product can be sticky and absorb into clothing. The dry borax may cause an allergic reaction. Use adequate ventilation and wash your hands after handling.**

3. Add 5 mL of the borax solution to the cup.

4. Stir until a solid forms in the cup.

5. Remove the solid with your hands. Place the substance on a paper towel. **Safety Alert: Do not taste any chemicals.**

6. Wait 2 to 3 minutes. The substance should not be sticky.

7. Test the borax putty for the physical properties listed in the table. Record your observations.

Making Borax Putty, continued

Physical Property	Observations
mass (g)	
roll into ball and wait 1 minute	
flatten into thin sheet and hold by one end	
roll into thick rope and pull apart slowly	
roll into thick rope and pull apart quickly	
roll into ball and drop on table	

8. Store your putty in a plastic bag.

Cleanup/Disposal

Wash the glassware, and return all materials. Clean your work area,
and wash your hands.

Analysis

1. What physical properties did you observe when you tested your borax
   putty? _____

2. Which physical properties are qualitative? _____

3. Which physical properties are quantitative? _____

Conclusions

1. What other information would you need to calculate the density of
   borax putty? _____

2. What observations would lead you to classify the substance as a solid?

   _____

3. What observations would lead you to classify the substance as a
   liquid? _____

Explore Further

Like so many science discoveries, borax putty was an "accident." Do
research to find out what scientists were actually trying to make when
they mixed glue (polyvinyl acetate) with borax (sodium borate).

Foul Water Mixture

Do you think the water that you drink is a substance or a mixture? Pure water is very expensive. Local agencies are responsible for safe tap water that is good tasting and inexpensive. A series of filtering steps converts wastewater into drinkable tap water. In this investigation, three of these processes will be used to filter a water mixture.

Materials   safety goggles   250-mL beaker
                  lab coat or apron   polystyrene cup
                  gravel   foul water mixture
                  sand   250-mL Erlenmeyer flask
                  100-mL graduated cylinder   paper clip

Procedure

1. Put on safety goggles and a lab coat or apron.

2. Observe the foul water mixture (mixture 1). Record the physical properties listed in the data table below.

Mixtures	Volume (mL)	Color of Mixture	Cloudiness of Mixture	Solids in Mixture
mixture 1: before treatment				
mixture 2: after separation by density				
mixture 3: after filtration				

3. Use the graduated cylinder to collect 100 mL of foul water. **Safety Alert: Handle glass with care. Report any broken or chipped glass to your teacher immediately. Wipe up all spills immediately.**

4. Tap the graduated cylinder gently to allow the particles to settle out by density. Wait 1 minute.

Foul Water Mixture, continued

5. Record the volume and physical properties of your sample (mixture 2).

6. Straighten out part of the paper clip. Use it to poke several small holes in the bottom of the cup. **Safety Alert: Take care not to poke or cut your hand.**

7. Add a 1-cm layer of gravel in the cup.

8. Add a 2-cm layer of sand on top of the gravel layer.

9. Add a 1-cm layer of gravel on top of the sand layer.

10. Hold the cup over the beaker. Gently pour the mixture into the cup. Catch the filtered water in the beaker as it drains.

11. Pour the filtered water back into the graduated cylinder. Record the volume and physical properties of the filtered water (mixture 3).

Cleanup/Disposal

Wash the glassware, and return all materials. Clean your work area, and wash your hands.

Analysis

1. Compare mixture 1 and mixture 3.

   _____

2. How do you know that the substances in the mixture were not chemically combined?

   _____

   _____

Conclusions

1. Was mixture 1 homogeneous or heterogeneous? Explain your answer.

   _____

   _____

   _____

Foul Water Mixture, continued

2. Was mixture 2 homogeneous or heterogeneous? Explain your answer.

_____

_____

3. Was mixture 3 homogeneous or heterogeneous? Explain your answer.

_____

_____

4. Calculate the percent of original foul water you recovered as treated water. _____
Use this formula:

$$\left(\frac{\text{final water volume}}{\text{initial water volume}}\right)100\%$$

Explore Further

Small amounts of substances, such as metals and salts, still exist in your treated water. What additional treatment steps might remove these substances from your water?

_____

_____

_____

One Substance or a Mixture?

Use with Investigation 2, pages 62–63

Using a process called paper chromatography, a mixture on a piece of paper can be separated. A solvent moves from one end of the paper to the other, causing different substances in the mixture to travel different distances. Does the ink in a pen or marker consist of one substance or a mixture? In this investigation, you will use paper chromatography to find out.

Materials   safety goggles   ruler
            lab coat or apron   watch glass or glass plate
            clear pint jar
            ethanol-water mixture
            10 cm × 10 cm piece of filter paper
            pen or marker with black water-soluble ink
            pen or marker with another color of water-soluble ink

Procedure

1. Put on safety goggles and a lab coat or apron.

2. Make a very light pencil line about 3 cm from one edge of the filter paper. Fold the paper and the pencil line in half, as shown. Unfold the paper.

3. Place a very small dot of black ink from the pen or marker on the left side of the pencil line, as shown. Use the other pen or marker to place a small ink dot on the right side of the line.

4. Pour about 1 cm of the ethanol-water mixture into the jar. Fold the paper along the fold line. Carefully lower it into the jar so it stands upright.

5. Gently place the watch glass or glass plate over the jar to seal it. **Safety Alert: Handle glass with care. Report any broken or chipped glass to your teacher immediately.**

6. Observe what happens as the solvent soaks upward through the paper.

7. When the solvent reaches 1 cm from the top, remove the paper. Let it dry.

8. Record your observations. Describe what happened in step 6. Describe the appearance of the dried filter paper.

One Substance or a Mixture?, continued

Cleanup/Disposal

Pour the solvent down the drain with plenty of running water. Rinse the jar with clean water, and return all materials. Keep the filter paper with your written observations. Wash your hands.

Analysis

1. Compare the chromatography results of the two inks on your filter paper.

_____

2. How does your filter paper compare with the results of your classmates?

_____

Conclusions

1. Was the black ink a single substance or a mixture? Explain.

_____

2. Was the other ink a single substance or a mixture? Explain.

_____

3. What can you conclude about the composition of these water-soluble inks?

_____

Explore Further

Use paper chromatography to analyze the colored shells of chocolate candies. Find out if they are mixtures. Use a 0.1% salt solution as a solvent. Use toothpicks dipped in water to dissolve and remove a tiny piece of colored shell from several candies of different colors.

Comparing Elements and Compounds

Use with Discovery Investigation 2, pages 77–78

Iron and sulfur can be stirred together to make a simple mixture.
These two elements also can combine chemically to form the
compound iron(II) sulfide. How do the properties of a compound
differ from the properties of its elements?

Materials
safety goggles
lab coat or apron
gloves
bar magnet
conductivity tester
iron strip
piece of solid sulfur
small paper plate

4 self-sealing plastic bags, each
containing one of the following:
   iron filings
   sulfur powder
   chunks of iron(II) sulfide
   mixture of powdered sulfur
     and iron filings

Procedure

1. Create a data table like the one shown at the bottom of the page.

2. Write a procedure to test the four kinds of matter for the properties
   listed in the table. Include at least one hypothesis and safety alerts.
   Use only the materials listed. Do not remove the iron filings, sulfur
   powder, or the mixture from their bags. The figure on the next page
   shows how to set up the conductivity test.

Sample of Matter	Bendable or Brittle?	Color and Appearance	Magnetic?	Conducts Electricity?	Metal or Nonmetal?
iron					
sulfur					
iron(II) sulfide					
mixture					

Comparing Elements and Compounds, continued

3. Have your procedure approved by your teacher.

4. Put on safety goggles, gloves, and a lab coat or apron.

5. Carry out your experiment. Record your observations and results in the table.

Cleanup/Disposal

Return all materials. Clean your work area, and wash your hands.

Analysis

1. Compare the appearance and color of iron, sulfur, and iron(II) sulfide.

_____

2. What evidence tells you if the elements are metals or nonmetals?

_____

3. Are the properties of the mixture most like those of the elements or iron(II) sulfide? Explain.

_____

4. What properties of iron(II) sulfide differ from the properties of either iron or sulfur?

_____

Conclusions

1. Can iron and sulfur be broken down into simpler substances? Explain.

_____

2. How could you show someone that a mixture of iron and sulfur is not the same as a compound of iron and sulfur?

_____

3. What observations show that iron and sulfur atoms bond to form a new substance?

_____

_____

Comparing Elements and Compounds, continued

Explore Further

Suppose you have a solvent that will dissolve sulfur, but not iron.
How could you use this solvent to separate an iron-sulfur mixture?
How could you reclaim the solid sulfur after separating the
mixture?

_____

_____

Express Lab 3

Use with Express Lab 3, page 89

Materials   safety goggles
lab coat or apron
stoppered test tube of dihydrogen monoxide
sucrose (table sugar)
spatula

Procedure

1. Put on safety goggles and a lab coat or apron.

2. Observe the appearance of dihydrogen monoxide. It is a molecular compound.

3. Remove the stopper from the test tube. Use your hand to sweep, or waft, the vapors from the compound toward your nose. Describe its odor. **Safety Alert: Do not directly smell any substance.**

4. Using the spatula, add a small amount of sucrose to the test tube. Replace the stopper, shake, and record what happens to the sugar.

Analysis

1. In the name *dihydrogen monoxide,* the prefix *di-* means "two." The prefix *mono-* means "one." Use the prefixes and element names to write the formula for this compound.

_____

2. What is the common name for dihydrogen monoxide?

_____

Polyatomic Ions in Reactions

Many polyatomic ions are part of compounds used to make foods, shampoo, makeup, and fertilizers. In this investigation, you will combine several pairs of ionic compounds. Which pairs will result in a chemical reaction?

Materials
safety goggles
lab coat or apron
well plate
0.05 M $AgNO_3$
0.2 M $Pb(NO_3)_2$

0.5 M $CaCl_2$
1.0 M Na_2CO_3
0.1 M Na_3PO_4
0.5 M $NaOH$
0.2 M Na_2SO_4

Procedure

1. Put on safety goggles and a lab coat or apron.

2. Add 5 drops of each compound to a well in a well plate as shown in the data table below. You will use 12 wells. **Safety Alert: Some chemicals are toxic. Do not get chemical on your skin or in your mouth. If this happens, report this to your teacher immediately.**

3. Record your observations, including any changes, in the table.

	Na_2CO_3 (CO_3^{2-})	Na_3PO_4 (PO_4^{3-})	NaOH (OH^2)	Na_2SO_4 (SO_4^{2-})
$AgNO_3$ Ag^+				
$Pb(NO_3)_2$ Pb^{2+}				
$CaCl_2$ Ca^{2+}				

Polyatomic Ions in Reactions, continued

Cleanup/Disposal

Rinse the well plate in the sink with plenty of running water, and return all materials. Clean your work area, and wash your hands.

Analysis

In the table below, use the observations from step 3 in the procedure and write the formula for any new compounds formed. If a reaction occurred, combine the cation and anion in bold using the criss-cross method. If no reaction occurred, do not write anything in the box.

	Na_2CO_3 anion is (CO_3^{2-})	Na_3PO_4 anion is (PO_4^{3-})	NaOH anion is (OH^{1-})	Na_2SO_4 anion is (SO_4^{2-})
$AgNO_3$ cation is Ag^{1+}				
$Pb(NO_3)_2$ cation is Pb^{2+}				
$CaCl_2$ cation is Ca^{2+}				

Conclusions

1. Which cation reacted the fewest number of times? _____

2. Which polyatomic ion reacted the fewest number of times? _____

Explore Further

Look at some food labels in your kitchen. Find some compound names on the back. Determine the cations and anions in the compounds, based on their names.

Writing Formulas of Ionic Compounds

Use with Investigation 3, pages 108–109

Cations and anions are charged particles. One kind of cation
and one kind of anion combine to form an ionic compound.
They combine in a certain ratio so the positive charges cancel
the negative charges. How do you determine this ratio? In this
investigation, you will practice combining ions to make neutral
compounds.

Materials   55 small blank cards
              pen with red ink
              pen with blue ink

Procedure

1. For each cation below, use the blue pen to make three cards. For
   example, write K^{1+} on three cards. Do the same for the anions using
   the red pen.

Cations
K^{1+}
NH_4^{1+}
Mg^{2+}
Cu^{1+}
Cu^{2+}
Fe^{2+}
Fe^{3+}
Sn^{2+}
Sn^{4+}

Anions
S^{2-}
F^{1-}
NO_3^{1-}
ClO_4^{1-}
CO_3^{2-}
SO_4^{2-}
PO_4^{3-}

2. Select one cation and one anion. Combine their cards to find the
   simplest neutral compound with a total ionic charge of zero. For
   example, combining two K^{1+} cards with one S^{2-} card gives a total
   charge of $(1+) + (1+) + (2-) = 0$.

Writing Formulas of Ionic Compounds, continued

3. Make a data table like the one below. In the first two columns, record the two ions you selected. In the last two columns, write the formula and name of the ionic compound.

Cation	Anion	Formula Unit	Compound Name
K^{1+}	S^{2-}	K_2S	potassium sulfide

4. Repeat steps 2 and 3 until you have recorded at least 25 different ionic compounds. Use every ion on the list at least once. If you need more than three cards for any of the ions, use the extra blank cards to make them.

Cleanup/Disposal

Return all materials.

Analysis

1. Why do cations and anions combine to form compounds that have no electric charge?

_____

2. Give the formula and name of a compound for which you had to make extra cards.

_____

3. Which cations required Roman numerals in compound names?

_____

Conclusions

1. Suppose cation X has a 2+ charge and anion Z has a 1− charge. Write the formula of the ionic compound of X and Z. _____

2. Suppose cation X has a 2+ charge and anion Z has a 3− charge. Write the formula of the ionic compound of X and Z. _____

3. Suppose cation X has a 3+ charge and anion Z has a 2− charge. Write the formula of the ionic compound of X and Z. _____

Writing Formulas of Ionic Compounds, continued

Explore Further

Write formulas for the following ionic compounds.

1. antimony(V) oxide _____

2. arsenic(V) sulfide _____

3. chromium(VI) oxide _____

4. manganese(VII) oxide _____

Anions in Chemical Reactions

Anions in column 17 of the periodic table contain very reactive elements. Four of these anions are found as compounds in the human body. Small amounts of sodium fluoride strengthen teeth. Sodium chloride is important for water regulation. Sodium bromide is needed in body tissues. Sodium iodide is needed to keep the thyroid gland working correctly. How do you think these anions will act when combined with cations? You will find out in this investigation.

Materials
safety goggles	0.1 M KI
lab coat or apron	0.2 M KBr
well plate	0.4 M KCl
0.05 M $AgNO_3$	0.4 M KF
0.2 M $Pb(NO_3)_2$	

Procedure

1. Put on safety goggles and a lab coat or apron.

2. Add 5 drops of each of the 8 compounds listed in the data table to a well in a well plate. You will use 8 wells. **Safety Alert: Some chemicals are toxic. Do not get chemicals on your skin or in your mouth. If this happens, report this to your teacher immediately.**

	KF	KCl	KBr	KI
$AgNO_3$				
$Pb(NO_3)_2$				

3. Record your observations, including any changes, in the table.

Anions in Chemical Reactions, continued

Cleanup/Disposal

Rinse the well plate in the sink with plenty of running water, and return all materials. Clean your work area, and wash your hands.

Analysis

1. In the table below, use the observations from number 2 and write the formula for any new compounds formed. If a reaction occurred, combine the cation and anion in bold using the criss-cross method. If no reaction occurred do not write anything in the box.

	KF anion is F^-	KCl anion is Cl^-	KBr anion is Br^-	KI anion is I^-
$AgNO_3$ cation is Ag+				
$Pb(NO_3)_2$ cation is Pb^{2+}				

Conclusions

1. Which anion(s) did not react with the silver cation? _____

2. Which anion(s) did not react with the lead cation? _____

3. Which anion made the most colorful changes? _____

Explore Further

Design an experiment to determine how the anions above will react with different chemicals such as nitric acid or bleach.

Comparing Ionic and Molecular Compounds

Use with Discovery Investigation 3, pages 117–118

Sodium chloride (table salt) and copper(II) sulfate are ionic compounds. Sucrose (table sugar) and ethanol are molecular compounds. How do the properties of ionic compounds differ from the properties of molecular compounds? You will find out in this investigation.

Materials safety goggles   4 100-mL beakers
       lab coat or apron   distilled water
       conductivity tester 50-mL graduated cylinder
       5-g samples of sodium spatula
        chloride, copper(II) stirring rod
        sulfate, sucrose, and 3 small crucibles
        ethanol   tongs
       hand lens   hot plate

Procedure

1. Make a data table like the one shown here.

Property	Sodium Chloride, NaCl	Copper(II) Sulfate, $CuSO_4$	Sucrose, $C_{12}H_{22}O_{11}$	Ethanol, C_2H_5OH

2. Put on safety goggles and a lab coat or apron.

3. Examine each sample. Use the hand lens if needed. Write your observations in the first two rows of the table.

Comparing Ionic and Molecular Compounds, continued

4. Write a procedure to test each compound for the properties described in the last three rows of the table. Use only the materials listed. (Ethanol is a liquid so it does not require a melting test.) Include hypotheses and safety alerts.

5. Have your procedure approved by your teacher.

6. Carry out your procedure, recording your results in the data table.

Cleanup/Disposal

Pour all solutions down the drain with plenty of running water. Wash the glassware and return all equipment. Clean your work area and wash your hands.

Analysis

1. Compare the appearances of the three solids. Can you use these observations to separate them into ionic and molecular compounds? _____

2. Which compounds conduct electricity? Which ones conduct electricity when dissolved in water? _____

3. Which solid melts at a warm temperature? _____

Conclusions

1. Compare the melting points of ionic compounds and molecular compounds.

2. Did the conductivity testing of the compounds identify them as molecular or ionic? Explain your answer. _____

3. A solution conducts electricity only if it has charged particles that are free to move. What can you conclude about the particles in each of the four solutions? _____

Explore Further

You also observed the properties of a third molecular compound in this lab. What is it, and what are its properties? How do you know if it conducts electricity? _____

_____

_____

Express Lab 4

Use with Express Lab 4, page 135

Materials   safety goggles
20 identical marbles
plastic bowl
balance

Procedure

1. Put on safety goggles. Measure and record the mass of the empty bowl.

2. Measure the mass of the bowl with 5 marbles. Calculate the total mass of the 5 marbles.

3. Repeat step 2 with 10 marbles and then with 20 marbles.

4. Draw a graph of marble mass versus marble number.

Analysis

1. Use your graph to estimate the mass of 5,000 marbles.

   _____

2. Suppose you had 6.02×10^{23} marbles. What would their total mass be?

   _____

3. How are the atoms in 1 mol of an element like the marbles in this lab?

   _____

Moles of Chalk

The mole is a counting unit in chemistry. A baker uses the word *dozen* to mean 12 items. Chemists use the word mole to mean 6.02×10^{23} particles. Have you ever used a mole of a substance? In this investigation, you will calculate how many moles of chalk are needed to write your name.

Materials   safety goggles
lab coat or apron
piece of chalk (calcium carbonate)
chalkboard
digital balance

Procedure

1. Put on safety goggles and a lab coat or apron.

2. Find the mass of the chalk using the digital balance. Record this in your data table below.

Chalk Sample	Mass(g)	Moles(mol)	Number of Particles (molecules)
chalk piece before writing			
estimate of chalk used			
chalk piece after writing			
actual chalk used			

3. Estimate how many grams of chalk are needed to write your name on the chalkboard. Record your estimate.

4. Write your name on the chalkboard with your chalk.

5. Measure and record the mass of your chalk.

6. Calculate and record the mass of chalk used to write your name.

Moles of Chalk, continued

Cleanup/Disposal

Return all materials. Clean your work area, and wash your hands.

Analysis

1. What is the chemical formula for calcium carbonate? _____

2. What is its molar mass in grams? _____

3. Convert the mass of your chalk before writing in the number of moles and particles. Record these values. _____

4. Convert the mass of calcium carbonate from your estimate into the number of moles and particles. Record these values. _____

5. Convert the mass of calcium carbonate after writing into the number of moles and particles. Record these values. _____

6. Convert the mass of the actual calcium carbonate used into the number of moles and particles. Record these values. _____

Conclusions

1. Compare your estimate in moles to the actual number of moles you used.

2. Calculate the percent error of your estimate. _____

The formula for percent error is:

$$\text{percent error} = \frac{\text{difference between estimated moles and accurate moles}}{\text{accurate moles}} \times 100\,\%$$

3. Why would it be difficult to complete this investigation using a pen or pencil?

_____

_____

Explore Further

Based on the number of particles (formula units) in your piece of chalk, estimate how many particles are in three other substances, such as an ice cube, a cube of sugar, and a shaker of salt.

Concentrations of Copper(II) Sulfate Solutions

Use with Investigation 4, pages 148–149

Can you tell the concentration of a solution just by looking at it? In this investigation, you will observe how solution color varies with solute concentration. You will use this information to estimate the concentration of an unknown solution.

Materials   safety goggles
            lab coat or apron
            5 250-mL beakers
            balance
            spatula
            60.0 g copper sulfate pentahydrate ($CuSO_4 \cdot 5H_2O$)
            100-mL graduated cylinder
            distilled water
            glass stirring rod

Procedure

1. Put on safety goggles and a lab coat or apron.

2. Place a clean, empty beaker on the balance. Measure and record its mass. Keep the beaker on the balance.

3. Using the spatula, begin to add very small amounts of copper sulfate to the beaker. Stop when the mass is 1.0 g more than the mass of the beaker alone. Record the mass of the beaker and copper sulfate.

4. Carefully measure 100 mL of distilled water using the graduated cylinder.

5. Add the water to the beaker. Stir the solution with the stirring rod until the copper sulfate is completely dissolved. Set the solution aside. **Safety Alert: Be careful with glassware, especially the stirring rod. Report any chipped or broken glass to your teacher.**

6. Repeat steps 2 through 5 three more times, except use 5.0 g, 10.0 g, and 20.0 g of copper sulfate. Label the four beakers. **Safety Alert: Do not taste any of the solutions.**

Concentrations of Copper Sulfate Solutions, continued

7. Prepare a fifth solution with the same concentration as one of the other solutions. Record the mass of copper sulfate in this solution. Do not label the beaker. Give this solution to another student or group to analyze.

8. Analyze the unknown solution you are given. Compare its color to the four solutions you prepared. Estimate how much copper sulfate is in the unknown solution. Record your estimate.

Cleanup/Disposal

Pour the copper sulfate solutions into a proper waste container. Wash and dry the glassware. Return all equipment, then wash your hands.

Analyis

1. What is the molar mass of copper sulfate pentahydrate? Use the formula $CuSO_4 \cdot 5H_2O$. (This substance contains 1 $CuSO_4$ formula unit and 5 water molecules.) _____

2. How many moles are in 1 g of the solute? _____

3. How many moles of solute are in each of the solutions you prepared?

_____

4. What is the molarity of each of these four solutions?

_____

Conclusions

1. How does the solution's appearance vary with concentration?

_____

2. What was your estimate of the unknown concentration?

_____

3. How did you determine your estimate?

_____

Explore Further

Do a similar investigation by preparing 0.4-*M*, 0.2-*M*, 0.1-*M*, and 0.05-*M* solutions in 500-mL volumetric flasks.

Percent Composition of a Compound

Percent composition is the percent by mass of each element in
a compound. The percent composition of an actual compound
is often difficult to calculate. In this investigation, you will use
"vegium" as a model for a compound. Vegium is a combination of
several dried vegetables. What will be the percent composition of
vegium?

Materials   safety goggles
                lab coat or apron
                digital balance
                plastic cup
                calculator
                vegium sample
                paper towel

Procedure

1. Put on safety goggles and a lab coat or apron.

2. Obtain a sample of vegium. Observe its physical properties. **Safety
Alert: Never eat any food substance used during an investigation.**

3. Make a hypothesis of which element in the vegium has the highest
percent composition by mass.

4. Spread the sample onto the paper towel. Separate it into its different
elements.

5. Place the paper cup on the balance. Press the tare button. The display
should read 0.00. The balance will ignore the mass of the cup. Do not
remove the cup.

Percent Composition of a Compound, continued

6. Measure the mass of each element and record this in the data table.
Add these masses to get the mass of your vegium sample.

Substance	Mass (g)
cornium (corn) in sample	
beanium (beans) in sample	
peaium (peas) in sample	
total vegium sample	

Cleanup/Disposal

Return all materials. Clean your work area, and wash your hands.

Analysis

1. Calculate the percent composition by mass of the cornium.

_____

2. Calculate the percent composition by mass of the beanium.

_____

3. Calculate the percent composition by mass of the peaium.

_____

Conclusions

1. When you add the percentages of each element, what should be the
total? _____

2. Add the percentages of cornium, beanium, and peaium together. What
is the total? _____

Percent Composition of a Compound, continued

Explore Further

You can make up a "chemical formula" for vegium in the following way:

1. Choose real elements from the periodic table to represent each vegetable in vegium. The heavy, large dried vegetables should be represented by heavy, large elements.

_____

_____

2. Using the molar mass for each real element, calculate the number of moles of each element in your sample.

_____

_____

3. Write a rough chemical formula for vegium using the mole amounts as subscripts. Fraction or decimal amounts are okay.

_____

_____

4. Divide each subscript by the smallest subscript. Are the new subscripts close to whole numbers? If not, double the subscripts. Rewrite your chemical formula using these subscripts in the simplest whole-number mole ratio. You now have the empirical formula for vegium!

_____

_____

The Formula of a Hydrate

Use with Discovery Investigation 4, pages 167–168

Water molecules combine with certain ionic compounds to form hydrates. Heating a hydrate removes the water, leaving the compound. How can you find the number of water molecules combined with one formula unit in an unknown hydrate?

Materials   safety goggles
lab coat or apron
tongs
crucible and lid
balance
sample of unknown hydrate
ring stand
iron ring
clay triangle
Bunsen burner

Procedure

1. Put on safety goggles and a lab coat or apron.

2. Set up the ring stand, iron ring, clay triangle, and burner as shown below. Adjust the ring height so the burner flame will just touch the crucible.

3. Be sure the crucible and lid are clean and dry. Place them on the balance and record their mass. Place the sample in the crucible. Record the mass of the sample, crucible, and lid. Find the mass of the sample. **Safety Alert: Do not touch or taste any substances.**

4. Use the tongs to place the crucible containing the hydrate on the clay triangle. Place the cover on the crucible so that the cover is slightly off-center. Light the burner.

5. Heat the crucible gently over the burner for 15 minutes. Turn off the burner. Use the tongs to place the crucible cover completely over the crucible. Let the crucible cool for 7 to 10 minutes. **Safety Alert: Do not touch the heated crucible with your hands.**

The Formula of a Hydrate, continued

6. Use the tongs to place the crucible, lid, and contents on the balance.
Record the mass. Find the mass of the contents.

Cleanup/Disposal

Put the contents of the crucible in the proper waste container. Wash and dry
the crucible. Return all equipment. Then wash your hands.

Analysis

1. What is the mass difference between the hydrate and the ionic
compound? What does this mass represent?

_____

_____

2. To determine the formula of the hydrate, what piece of information
do you need? Ask your teacher for this information.

_____

_____

3. What is the empirical formula of the hydrate? Show your work.

_____

_____

Conclusions

1. Suppose the heating did not remove all of the water from the hydrate.
How would this affect your results? _____

2. List at least two other possible sources of error in this investigation. _____

Explore Further

A desiccant is a compound used to absorb moisture from the air. How could
the formula of a hydrate indicate its effectiveness as a desiccant?

_____

_____

Express Lab 5

Use with Express Lab 5, page 178

Materials   safety goggles
             lab coat or apron
             gloves
             25 mL of 0.1 *M* copper(II) chloride ($CuCl_2$)
             aluminum strip
             100-mL beaker

Procedure

1. Put on safety goggles, a lab coat or apron, and gloves.

2. Put the aluminum strip in the beaker. **Safety Alert: Be careful when working with glassware.**

3. Add the copper(II) chloride solution. **Safety Alert: Handle with care.**

4. Record your observations.

5. Put the solid waste in a proper waste container. Pour the solution down the drain with running water. Wash and return the beaker. Wash your hands.

Analysis

1. What did you observe during the reaction?

   _____

   _____

2. What were the reactants?

   _____

   _____

3. What product was formed?

   _____

   _____

Chemical Balancing Act

Glucose is a simple sugar. Upon heating, the glucose decomposes before reaching its boiling point. You may have experienced something like this when heating syrup and it burned. What do you think this decomposition reaction will look and smell like? In this investigation, you will observe both.

Materials   safety goggles
lab coat or apron
disposable test tube
test tube holder
1.0 g of glucose ($C_6H_{12}O_6$)
cobalt chloride paper
test tube rack
Bunsen burner
striker

Procedure

1. Put on safety goggles and a lab coat or apron.

2. Place 1 g of glucose in the test tube.

3. Light the burner with the striker. **Safety Alert: Use care around hot objects. Report any burns immediately.**

4. Use a test tube holder to place the test tube in the burner flame. Heat the bottom of the test tube. **Safety Alert: Be sure the test tube is facing away from you and other people.**

5. Observe the test tube as you heat it. In the table below, describe what happens at the bottom and at the mouth of the tube.

Location	Observation of Changes
bottom of the test tube	
mouth of the test tube	

Chemical Balancing Act, continued

6. Turn the Bunsen burner off. Allow the test tube to cool.

7. Touch the cobalt chloride paper to the liquid at the mouth of the test tube. If the liquid is water, the paper will change from blue to pink. **Safety Alert: Some chemicals are toxic. Do not get chemical on your skin or in your mouth. If this happens, report it immediately.**

Cleanup/Disposal

Dispose of the glassware in a waste container. Return all materials. Clean your work area, and wash your hands.

Analysis

1. What color did the cobalt chloride paper turn? Was water vapor present?

_____

2. Write the balanced chemical equation for the decomposition of glucose into water and carbon.

_____

3. What was the black substance in the bottom of the test tube? (Hint: Look at the chemical equation.)

_____

Conclusions

1. Calculate the molar mass of each reactant and product in the reaction. _____

_____

2. Calculate the initial moles of glucose.

_____

Explore Further

Think of three other decomposition reactions that occur in your everyday life. Compare your ideas with others.

Candle Combustion and Conservation of Matter

A combustion reaction involves the burning of matter in the presence of oxygen. When a substance is burned, its matter is not destroyed. It may seem like the substance just disappeared, but the matter was changed into new matter. In this investigation, you will observe a candle during a combustion reaction. If the candle isn't destroyed, where does it go?

Materials
safety goggles	glass plate
lab coat or apron	calculator
digital balance	candle
matches	

Procedure

1. Put on safety goggles and a lab coat or apron.

2. Measure and record the mass of the glass plate.

Object	Mass (g)
glass plate	
glass plate and candle before burning	
candle before burning	
glass plate and candle after burning	
candle after burning	
portion of candle that burned	

3. Light the candle and drip a little wax onto the plate. Blow out the candle and stick it onto the plate. **Safety Alert: Use care around hot objects. Report any burns immediately.**

4. Measure and record the mass of the glass plate with the candle.

5. Calculate and record the mass of the candle by subtracting the mass of the glass plate.

6. Light the candle and allow it to burn for 3 minutes.

7. Gently blow out the candle so wax does not splatter.

8. Measure and record the mass of the candle and glass plate without losing any wax.

Candle Combustion and Conservation of Matter, continued

9. Calculate and record the mass of the candle by subtracting the mass of the glass plate.

10. Calculate and record the mass of the candle that burned in 3 minutes.

Cleanup/Disposal

Wash the glassware, and return all materials. Clean your work area, and wash your hands.

Analysis

1. How do you know that you observed a combustion reaction?

_____

_____

2. Balance this equation for the burning of wax, $C_{25}H_{52}$.

_____$C_{25}H_{52}(s) +$ _____ $O_2(g) \rightarrow$ _____ $CO_2(g) +$ _____ $H_2O(g)$

3. Based on the reaction above, what products formed when the candle burned?

_____

4. What law is demonstrated by balanced chemical equations?

_____

Conclusions

What happened to the mass of the candle during the investigation?
Explain your answer. _____

_____

Explore Further

Respiration is one type of combustion reaction. It involves the burning of carbohydrates. Look at the nutrition labels on foods like rice, beans, and pasta. Compare the grams of carbohydrate to the number of calories.

▇▶ Chemistry

The Decomposition of Basic Copper(II) Carbonate

Use with Investigation 5, pages 194–195

In a decomposition reaction, a compound is broken down
into smaller products. How can you tell when a decomposition
reaction takes place? In this investigation, you will observe the
decomposition of basic copper(II) carbonate.

Materials safety goggles
lab coat or apron
porcelain evaporating dish
balance
spatula
5.0 g of basic copper(II) carbonate ($CuCO_3 \cdot Cu(OH)_2$)
ring stand
ring clamp
Bunsen burner
tongs
glass stirring rod

Procedure

1. Put on safety goggles and a lab coat or apron.

2. Measure and record the mass of a clean, dry evaporating dish.

3. Use the spatula to add between 1.0 g and 5.0 g of basic
   copper(II) carbonate to the dish.

4. Measure and record the mass of the dish and reactant. Find the
   mass of the reactant. Write a description of this solid.

5. Set up the ring stand and clamp as shown. Place the burner
   below the ring so its flame will just touch the dish.

6. Place the dish on the ring. Light the burner. **Safety Alert: Do
   not touch heated objects with your hands. Keep clothing and
   hair away from open flames.**

7. Heat the dish over a medium flame. Stir the reactant gently
   with the glass rod. Turn off the burner when the reactant has
   entirely changed color from green to black.

The Decomposition of Basic Copper(II) Carbonate, continued

8. Let the dish cool for 7 to 10 minutes. Write a description of the product.

9. Use the tongs to place the dish and product on the balance. Measure and record the mass. Find the mass of the product.

Cleanup/Disposal

Put the cooled product in the proper waste container. Wash and dry the dish and stirring rod. Return all equipment. Then wash your hands.

Analysis

1. Use the reactant's mass and formula to find the number of moles of reactant.

_____

_____

2. The product is copper(II) oxide, CuO. Use its mass and formula to find the number of moles of product.

_____

_____

3. What is the mole ratio of CuO to $CuCO_3 \cdot Cu(OH)_2$?

_____

_____

The Decomposition of Basic Copper(II) Carbonate, continued

Conclusions

1. How do your descriptions of the reactant and product tell you that a reaction has occurred?

   _____

   _____

2. How do the reactant and product masses tell you that a decomposition reaction has occurred?

   _____

   _____

3. What do you think is the unbalanced equation for the decomposition reaction?

   _____

   _____

4. From the mole ratio you calculated, what is the balanced equation? (Hint: The coefficients in a balanced equation represent moles.)

   _____

   _____

Explore Further

Use your results and the balanced equation for the reaction to calculate the mass of carbon dioxide produced.

_____

_____

Using the Activity Series
Use with Discovery Investigation 5, pages 200–201

When an element is placed in an ionic solution, a single-replacement reaction may or may not occur. In this investigation, you will make several predictions and then design an experiment to test them. How can you predict which elements will react with which solutions?

Materials   safety goggles
lab coat or apron
16 reaction wells
4 eyedroppers
10 mL of 0.1 M aluminum nitrate ($Al(NO_3)_3$)
10 mL of 0.1 M copper(II) sulfate ($CuSO_4$)
10 mL of 0.1 M iron(II) sulfate ($FeSO_4$)
10 mL of 0.1 M zinc nitrate ($Zn(NO_3)_2$)
small strips of aluminum, copper, iron, and zinc

Procedure

1. Create a data table like the one shown.

Element	$Al(NO_3)_3$ Solution	$CuSO_4$ Solution	$FeSO_4$ Solution	$Zn(NO_3)_2$ Solution
Al				
Cu				
Fe				
Zn				

2. Predict which of the 16 combinations in the table will produce a chemical reaction. Indicate your predictions with small checkmarks.

3. Write a procedure to test each combination to determine if a reaction occurs. Use only the listed materials. Include safety alerts.

4. Have your procedure approved by your teacher.

5. Put on safety goggles and a lab coat or apron.

6. Carry out your experiment. Record your observations in the table.

Using the Activity Series, continued

Cleanup/Disposal

Put used and unused substances in the proper waste containers. Wash and return the equipment. Then wash your hands.

Analysis

1. Which of the four metals is the most reactive? Which is the least reactive?

_____

_____

2. Describe what happened when a metal was placed in a solution containing a compound of that metal (for example, zinc in zinc nitrate solution). Explain your observations.

_____

_____

Conclusions

1. What did you base your predictions on?

_____

2. Which of your predictions were supported by your results?

_____

3. If any predictions did not match your results, can you determine why? Explain.

_____

_____

Explore Further

Choose five other metals. Predict which of the four solutions will react with each metal.

_____

_____

Express Lab 6

Use with Express Lab 6, page 224

Materials   6 pennies
              2 nickels

Procedure

1. Examine the balanced equation for making ammonia from nitrogen and hydrogen:
$$N_2 + 3H_2 \rightarrow 2NH_3$$

2. Use coins to model the left side of this equation. Use nickels to represent nitrogen atoms and pennies to represent hydrogen atoms.

3. Rearrange the coins to model the two ammonia molecules on the right side of the equation.

Analysis

1. The coin models show the number of molecules of each substance in the reaction. They also show the number of moles of each substance. Why?

_____

_____

2. Write six mole ratios for this equation.

_____

_____

_____

_____

Percent Yield
Use with Investigation 6, pages 247–248

Magnesium burns to form magnesium oxide. You can predict
how much MgO should form. Then you can measure how much
actually forms. What is the percent yield?

Materials
safety goggles

lab coat or apron

75 cm of magnesium ribbon

crucible

tongs

balance

Bunsen burner

clay triangle

ring stand

ring clamp

eyedropper

glass stirring rod

distilled water

Procedure

1. To record your data, make a table like the one below.

Item	Mass (g)
empty crucible	
crucible and Mg ribbon	
Mg ribbon	
crucible and MgO	
MgO	

2. Put on safety goggles and a lab coat or apron.

3. Roll the magnesium into a ball that will fit in the crucible.

4. Find and record the masses of the first two items in the table.
Calculate and record the mass of the ribbon.

5. Set up the ring stand, ring clamp, and burner as shown. Place
the clay triangle on the ring. Place the crucible containing the
metal ball on the triangle.

6. Light the burner. Heat the crucible until the magnesium starts
to burn. **Safety Alert: Tie back long hair. Keep loose clothing
away from the flame. Do not look directly at the burning
magnesium.**

Percent Yield, continued

7. After all the magnesium burns, turn off the burner. Allow
the crucible to cool. Use the tongs to place the crucible on
the counter. With the eyedropper, slowly add about 1 mL of
distilled water to the crucible. Use the stirring rod to break up
the product and mix it with the water. Scrape any product off
the stirring rod so that it remains in the crucible.

8. Light the burner. Heat the crucible and its contents for at least
5 minutes until the mixture is dry. Turn off the burner. Allow
the crucible to cool.

9. Use the tongs to place the crucible with contents on the
balance. Record the mass of the crucible and MgO. Calculate
and record the mass of the MgO.

Cleanup/Disposal

Discard the solid in a waste container. Wash and dry the crucible
and stirring rod. Return all equipment. Then wash your hands.

Analysis

1. Write a balanced equation for this reaction. _____

2. What is the theoretical yield of MgO? _____

3. What is the actual yield of MgO? _____

Conclusions

1. What is the percent yield of MgO? _____

2. What might cause the percent yield to be less than 100%? _____

3. How do you think you might improve the percent yield? _____

_____

Explore Further

Zinc metal burns in air with a blue-green flame to form zinc oxide,
ZnO. If 2.00 g of zinc burns, what is the theoretical yield of ZnO?
What is the actual yield of ZnO if the percent yield is 86%?

_____

Modeling Limiting and Excess Reactants

The price of items you buy is based largely on the cost of making them. Manufacturers compete to reduce costs and increase profits. They try to increase the percent yield of their manufacturing processes by making the most products with the least waste. In this investigation, you will model a chemical reaction and determine the limiting and excess reactants.

Materials   safety goggles   20 metal paper clips (call these M)
                 plastic bag   20 colored paper clips (call these C)

Procedure

1. Join pairs of paper clips of the same color. Each pair represents a diatomic molecule. Place these molecules into the plastic bag. **Safety Alert: Handle glass with care.**

2. Without looking, choose 15 molecules from the plastic bag. Set the bag aside.

3. Line up the M_2 and C_2 molecules in two separate rows.

4. Suppose this reaction occurs: $M_2 + 3C_2 \rightarrow 2MC_3$. Group reactant molecules using the ratio of 1 M_2 to 3C_2. You may have leftover molecules.

5. Make the grouped molecules "react." Do this by taking them apart and forming two MC_3 molecules.

6. Continue making products until you run out of one of the reactants. Show your work to your teacher.

Cleanup/Disposal

Return all materials. Clean your work area, and wash your hands.

Analysis

1. How many molecules of each reactant did you draw from the bag? _____

2. How many molecules of the product did you form? _____

Modeling Limiting and Excess Reactants, continued

3. Which reactant did you run out of first? _____

4. How many molecules of each reactant were left over when you finished? _____

Conclusions

1. Compare your results with three other students. Create a chart to show these results.

2. Explain any similarities or differences between your results and the other students' results.

_____

_____

3. What is the maximum number of product molecules you can form from all the clips you were given? _____

4. If you could use all of the clips you were given, which reactant would be limiting? _____

Explore Further

You have probably experienced a real-life event in which something was limiting or in excess. Write a half-page paragraph describing your story.

Ideal Molar Ratios

Many reactions absorb or release heat as they occur. This temperature change can be used to follow a reaction's progress. It can be used to measure the amount of product formed. How big of a temperature change can occur during a chemical reaction? In this investigation, you will observe several temperature changes.

Materials   safety goggles   50-mL graduated cylinder
                lab coat or apron   thermometer
                glass stirring rod   60 mL of 1.0 M HCl
                3 polystyrene cups   60 mL of 1.0 M NaOH

Procedure

1. Put on safety goggles and a lab coat or apron.

2. Use the graduated cylinder to measure 30.0 mL of 1.0 M HCl. Pour it into the cup. **Safety Alert: Some chemicals are toxic. Do not get chemical on your skin or in your mouth. If this happens, report it immediately. Handle glass with care. Report any broken or chipped glass to your teacher immediately. Wipe up all spills immediately.**

Cup	Temperature of HCl Solution	Highest Temperature of HCl+NaOH
1		
2		
3		

3. Hold the thermometer in the solution for 1 minute. Record the temperature.

4. Add 10 mL of 1.0 M NaOH to the same cup. Gently stir the contents with the stirring rod.

5. Record the highest temperature the solution reaches.

6. Using a new cup, repeat steps 2 through 5 using 20.0 mL of HCl and 20.0 mL of NaOH.

7. Using a new cup, repeat steps 2 through 5 using 10.0 mL of HCl and 30.0 mL of NaOH.

Ideal Molar Ratios, continued

Cleanup/Disposal

Wash the glassware, and return all materials. Clean your work area, and wash your hands.

Analysis

1. Write the balanced chemical equation for the reaction between HCl*(aq)* and NaOH*(aq)*.

_____

2. Using the reaction above, what is the mole ratio of the reactants?

_____

3. In cup 1, was there an excess reactant? If so, which one?

_____

4. In cup 2, was there an excess reactant? If so, which one?

_____

5. In cup 3, was there an excess reactant? If so, which one?

_____

Conclusions

1. Which reaction had the greatest temperature change? Explain your answer.

_____

2. Which reaction produced the greatest amount of product? Explain your answer.

_____

3. Which reaction did not have a limiting reactant? Explain your answer.

_____

Explore Further

A recipe is a set of ideal ingredient ratios. Interview a family member. Ask them to describe a time when they made a measuring mistake while cooking. Which ingredient was the excess or limiting ingredient? What was the result? _____

Limiting Reactants
Use with Discovery Investigation 6, pages 255–256

Magnesium and hydrochloric acid react to form magnesium chloride and hydrogen. Given certain amounts of the reactants, how can you identify the limiting reactant? In this investigation, you will combine different amounts of magnesium with a fixed amount of acid.

Materials
safety goggles
lab coat or apron
3 500-mL Erlenmeyer flasks
grease pencil
100-mL graduated cylinder
240 mL of 1.0 M HCl
3.5 g of Mg ribbon
balance
3 large round balloons

Procedure

1. Read the following steps of the procedure. Write a paragraph describing what you expect to happen in this investigation. Predict differences among the three flasks.

2. Design and draw a table to record your observations and any important data.

3. Put on safety goggles and a lab coat or apron.

4. Use the grease pencil to label the flasks 1, 2, and 3.

5. Add 80 mL of hydrochloric acid to each flask. **Safety Alert: Do not let the acid contact your skin or clothing. Alert your teacher immediately if any acid spills.**

6. Cut pieces of magnesium ribbon so that you have a 0.5-g sample, a 1.0-g sample, and a 2.0-g sample.

7. Place 0.5 g of magnesium in a balloon. Stretch the neck of the balloon over the top of flask 1, keeping the metal in the balloon. Do the same for the 1.0-g sample and 2.0-g sample, as shown.

Limiting Reactants, continued

8. Lift up each balloon so the magnesium drops into the acid. Keep the balloons on the flasks. Observe what happens. Record your observations.

Cleanup/Disposal

Pour liquids down the drain with plenty of running water. Any remaining solids should be rinsed thoroughly with water in the flask and then put in the proper waste container. Wash and dry the glassware. Return all equipment. Wash your hands.

Analysis

1. Compare the volumes of gas produced in each reaction. _____

2. What did you observe in flask 3 that you did not see in the other flasks? _____

3. How did your observations compare with your predictions? _____

_____

Conclusions

1. What is the limiting reactant in flask 1? In flask 3? _____

2. What is in excess in flask 1? In flask 3? _____

3. Why can't you easily identify the limiting and excess reactants in flask 2? _____

Explore Further

Find the number of moles of magnesium in each sample. Find the number of moles in 80 mL of 1.0 M HCl. Use this information and a balanced equation to explain your results.

_____

_____

Express Lab 7

Use with Express Lab 7, page 267

Materials   household ammonia in a small plastic bottle with cap
perfume in a small plastic bottle with cap
timer or watch with second hand

Procedure

1. Have two classmates stand side by side about 2 m away from the bottle of ammonia. Remove the cap from the bottle and start the timer.

2. When both classmates can smell the ammonia, stop the timer and place the cap back on the bottle. Record the elapsed time.

3. When the ammonia smell has lessened, repeat steps 1 and 2 with the bottle of perfume.

Analysis

1. Compare the times for the observers to smell the ammonia and the perfume.

_____

_____

2. Which moves faster, gas particles of ammonia or gas particles of perfume?

_____

_____

Kinetic Theory in Action

Moving gas particles have kinetic energy. These particles travel in a straight line until they collide with another object. The oxygen molecules surrounding you right now are moving at about 400 meters per second. Can you visualize gas particles moving at this speed? In this investigation, you will see evidence of gas particle movement.

Materials
safety goggles
lab coat or apron
petri dish
cotton swabs
wax pencil
colored pencils (yellow, green, blue)
test tube rack
0.04% bromthymol blue (BTB)
1.0 M HCl
1.0 M NaHSO$_3$
0.5 M NaOH
1.0 M NH$_4$Cl

Procedure

1. Put on safety goggles and a lab coat or apron.

2. Open the petri dish. Place one small drop of bromthymol blue (BTB) wherever you see a black dot in the diagram below. Do not crowd the drops or let them touch. Quickly replace the lid after adding the drops.

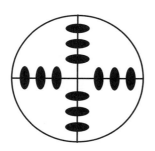

Kinetic Theory in Action, continued

3. Using the colored pencils, draw your observations of the BTB color changes in diagram 1.

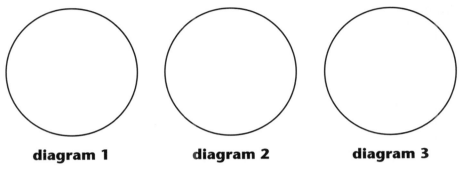

diagram 1   **diagram 2**   **diagram 3**

4. Open the lid. Place one small drop of HCl and one small drop of $NaHSO_3$ in the middle of the petri dish, one on top of the other. Quickly replace lid.

5. After 5 to 10 seconds, observe and record the color changes in diagram 2. Look closely from the top and sides. The drops may consist of two or three colors.

6. Observe and record the colors in the dish after the colors stop changing. Use diagram 3.

7. Open the lid of the dish. Carefully absorb the center mixture with a cotton swab. Do not absorb any of the BTB.

8. Open the lid. Place one small drop of NaOH and one small drop of NH_4Cl in the middle of the petri dish, one on top of the other. Quickly replace lid.

9. Repeat steps 5 and 6 with the new drops. Record your observations in diagrams 4 and 5.

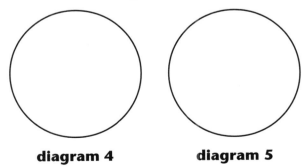

diagram 4   **diagram 5**

Kinetic Theory in Action, continued

Cleanup/Disposal

Wash the petri dish, and return all materials. Clean your work area, and wash your hands.

Analysis

1. Why did the drops closer to the center change before the drops near the edge?

_____

2. Why did the outside of a single drop change before the middle?

_____

3. How did the second part of the experiment ($NaOH$ and NH_4Cl) differ from the first?

_____

_____

Conclusions

1. The BTB changed even though you added nothing to it. Explain the changes you observed in terms of the chemical reactions that were occurring.

_____

_____

2. Explain how these experiments relate to the kinetic theory of molecular motion. You may need to reread the five assumptions of the theory. Decide how your observations support each part of the theory.

_____

_____

Explore Further

Design an experiment in which you could observe the effect of the size of the BTB drops. Find out if the rate at which the drops change is affected. Explain your results in terms of kinetic theory.

_____

The Deflating Balloon

Warm air is less dense than cooler air. Hot-air balloon pilots heat
the air inside their balloons to make it rise. If their balloon drifts
into colder air, the balloon will begin to shrink. Why does the
balloon shrink? In this investigation, you will find out.

Materials   safety goggles   hot plate
          lab coat or apron   balloon
          10-mL graduated cylinder   tongs
          250-mL Erlenmeyer flask   shallow pan

Procedure

1. Put on safety goggles and a lab coat or apron.

2. Add 10 mL of tap water to an Erlenmeyer flask. Place the flask
    on a hot plate and heat until the water boils. **Safety Alert: Hot
    water and glassware can burn you. Tell your teacher if you
    get burned.**

3. Use tongs to remove the hot flask from the hot plate. Quickly
    fit a balloon over the rim of the flask.

4. Return the flask to the hot plate.

5. Observe what happens to the balloon's volume when the water
    boils again. Record your observations in the table. **Safety
    Alert: Allow the balloon to inflate a small amount.**

Flask with Balloon	Volume Observations
after it is placed on the hot plate (step 4)	
after it is removed from the hot plate (step 6)	
after it is placed in a shallow pan of tap water (step 8)	

6. Remove the flask from the hot plate.

7. Observe and record what happens to the balloon's volume.

8. Place the flask in a shallow pan of tap water.

9. Observe and record what happens to the balloon's volume.

The Deflating Balloon, continued

Cleanup/Disposal

Wash the glassware, and return all materials. Clean your work area, and wash your hands.

Analysis

1. Explain the balloon's change in volume when the flask was placed on the hot plate.

_____

2. Explain the balloon's change in volume when the flask was removed from the hot plate.

_____

3. Explain the balloon's change in volume when the flask was placed in tap water.

_____

Conclusions

1. In order to test a gas law, gas needs to be trapped. What traps the gas in this investigation?

_____

2. Describe how Charles's law is related to this investigation.

_____

_____

3. What happened to the gas particles when the flask was placed in the pan of water? Explain your answer.

_____

_____

Explore Further

Scientists used Charles's law to invent refrigerants. Do research on the use of refrigerants in cooling devices such as household refrigerators.

The Volume and Temperature of a Gas
Use with Investigation 7, pages 285–286

How can you see the effect of a change in temperature on the volume of a gas? In this investigation, you will examine what happens to the volume of a sample of gas when its temperature changes.

Materials   safety goggles
lab coat or apron
2 pairs of rubber gloves
round balloon
black permanent marker
string
meter stick
2 buckets
ice water
warm water

Procedure

1. Use the data table below.

Temperature	Circumference (cm)
room temperature	
cold	
warm	

2. Put on safety goggles and a lab coat or apron.

3. Partially inflate the balloon, making sure it is not completely inflated. Tie it closed. Use the marker to make three dots equally spaced around the middle of the balloon. **Safety Alert: Be sure to wear safety goggles in case a balloon breaks.**

4. Use a piece of string to measure the circumference of the balloon. Place the string around the balloon so that it goes over all three dots. Mark this string length with your fingers. Measure this length on the meter stick and record it.

The Volume and Temperature of a Gas, continued

5. Place the ice water in one bucket. Put on rubber gloves and hold the balloon in the ice water for 10 minutes. With a partner, take turns holding the balloon in the water.

6. Remove the balloon. Quickly measure and record its circumference as in step 4.

7. Repeat steps 5 and 6 using warm water.

Cleanup/Disposal

Return or dispose of your materials. Wash your hands.

Analysis

1. What happened to the circumference of the balloon as it was cooled?

_____

2. What happened to the circumference of the balloon as it was warmed?

_____

3. Why doesn't the pressure of the gas in the balloon affect the results?

_____

Conclusions

1. When the circumference of the balloon increases, what happens to gas volume? Explain.

_____

_____

2. Based on your results, how is the volume of a gas affected by a change in temperature?

_____

_____

The Volume and Temperature of a Gas, continued

Explore Further

Design a similar investigation using different methods to cool and
warm the balloon. Have your teacher approve your procedure first.
Do your new results confirm your original results? Explain.

_____

_____

Temperature, Pressure, and Number of Gas Particles
Use with Discovery Investigation 7, pages 292–293

Gases have pressure because gas particles collide with their
container. If gas volume stays constant, a change in temperature
or the number of particles affects the pressure of a gas. How are
temperature, pressure, and number of particles related? In this
investigation, you will examine these properties for a sample of gas.

Materials   safety goggles   large plastic bowl
lab coat or apron   10-mL graduated cylinder
empty soft drink can   ice
hot plate   water
beaker tongs

Procedure

1. Read all of the steps of the procedure. Then proceed to step 2.

2. Predict what will happen when the top of the can is lowered
   into the ice water. Record your prediction.

3. Put on safety goggles and a lab coat or apron.

4. Pour 10 to 15 mL of water into the soft drink can. Place the
   can on the hot plate. Turn on the hot plate. Heat the can until
   steam comes out of the opening. **Safety Alert: Do not touch
   any hot objects. Keep the electrical cord of the hot plate away
   from water.**

5. While the water in the can is heating, fill the plastic bowl
   halfway with ice and water.

6. Using the tongs, quickly move the can over the ice water, then
   turn the can over and plunge the top of the can into the ice
   water. Record your observations.

Cleanup/Disposal

Return or dispose of your materials. Wash your hands.

Temperature, Pressure, and Number of Gas Particles, continued

Analysis

1. What happened to the gases in the can when they were cooled?

_____

_____

2. What happened to the can?

_____

_____

3. Describe the contents of the can after it cooled.

_____

_____

Conclusions

1. Explain what happened to the can. Include the importance of temperature and number of gas particles.

_____

_____

2. Compare your results with your predictions. Explain any differences.

_____

_____

Explore Further

At home, twist the cap onto an empty 1-L or 2-L plastic bottle at room temperature. Place the bottle in the freezer. Wait 10 minutes. Then remove the bottle and observe its appearance. Leave the cap on the bottle and allow it to warm up to room temperature. Observe what happens. Record your observations. Explain the changes that occurred in the bottle.

_____

_____

_____

Express Lab 8

Use with Express Lab 8, page 309

Materials   safety goggles
balloon
wool cloth
strip of newspaper, about 3 cm wide
small bits of paper

Procedure

1. Put on safety goggles.

2. Rub the balloon with the wool cloth.

3. Hold the strip of paper near the balloon. What happens?

4. Hold the strip just above the bits of paper. What happens?

Analysis

1. The balloon becomes electrically charged when rubbed. It attracts paper because opposite charges attract. The balloon and paper are matter, and matter is made of atoms. What do these observations tell you about atoms?

   _____

   _____

2. If the balloon is negatively charged, what kind of charge does it attract?

   _____

   _____

Evidence of Electrons

When you walk across a carpet on cold, dry days and touch another person, what happens? The shock you feel is called static electricity. You actually collect electrons as you walk. Your shoes sweep electrons off of the rug fibers. Have you ever seen electrons on the bottom of your shoes? In this investigation, you won't see electrons, but you will see evidence of electrons.

Materials   6 pieces of clear plastic tape, each 25 cm in length

Procedure

1. Firmly stick the six pieces of tape to a tabletop or countertop, leaving 2 to 3 cm hanging over the edge.

2. Grasp the free ends of two pieces of tape, one with each hand. Pull them upward quickly, peeling them from the tabletop.

3. Slowly bring the two pieces of tape near each other. Record your observations below. Throw the tape in a waste container.

Tape	Observations
two pieces peeled off table quickly (step 2)	
two pieces pulled through fingers (step 4)	
one piece peeled quickly and one pulled through fingers (step 8)	

4. Slowly pull one piece of tape through your thumb and forefinger. This will be sticky at first, but will become easier as you continue. Repeat with another piece of tape.

5. Slowly bring the two pieces of tape from step 4 near each other. Record your observations. Throw the tape in a waste container.

6. Use one piece of tape to repeat step 2.

7. Use the last piece of tape to repeat step 4.

8. Slowly bring the two pieces of tape from steps 6 and 7 near each other. Record your observations. Throw the tape in a waste container.

Evidence of Electrons, continued

Cleanup/Disposal

Wash your hands.

Analysis

1. Did the two pieces of tape peeled from the lab table have the same or opposite charges? Explain your answer.

_____

2. Did the two pieces of tape pulled through your fingers have the same or opposite charges? Explain your answer.

_____

3. Did the pieces of tape in step 8 have the same or opposite charges? Explain your answer.

_____

4. Which pieces had a positive charge? Which pieces had a negative charge?

_____

Conclusions

Explain how this investigation proves the existence of particles too small for your eye to see.

_____

_____

Explore Further

Around 400 B.C., Democritus hypothesized the existence of atoms. More than 2,000 years later, Dalton published his atomic theory. Neither of these men actually saw atoms. Research how the scanning tunneling microscope changed the way atoms are visualized.

Rutherford Boxes

We often forget that early scientists worked without the benefit of high-powered microscopes. They relied on relatively crude tools, an active imagination, and the scientific method. Rutherford and other scientists worked with what some people call a "black box." They called it a black box because, even though Rutherford could not see the atom, he described a portion of it. Have you tried to describe something you couldn't see?

Materials   safety goggles
1-in foam board
scissors
tape
box with a lid
1 piece of plain paper
pen

Procedure

1. Put on safety goggles.

2. Cut a capital letter from a piece of 1-in foam board. Do not let other students see your letter.

3. Tape the letter onto the inside bottom of the box.

4. Place one marble in the box. Place the lid on the box.

5. Exchange boxes with another student.

6. Without opening the box, carefully tilt the box so the marble moves around the letter for one minute. Record your observations below (trial 1).

Trial	Observations
1	
2	
3	

Rutherford Boxes, continued

7. Record your observations after moving the box for another minute (trial 2).

8. Record your observations after moving the box for one more minute (trial 3).

9. Do not open the box.

Cleanup/Disposal

Return all materials. Clean your work area, and wash your hands.

Analysis

1. Before opening the box, what letter do you think is inside?

   _____

2. Open the box. Was your guess correct? If not, was your guess close to the same shape as the letter in the box?

   _____

3. What other things could you have done with the box to guess the correct letter?

   _____

Conclusions

1. How is this like Rutherford's gold foil experiment?

   _____

   _____

2. How would your results be different if the letter and the marble had positive charges?

   _____

   _____

Explore Further

Radar equipment used by ships and submarines is similar to Rutherford's experiment. Research the discovery and use of radar to detect unknown objects in the ocean.

Atoms and Isotopes
Use with Investigation 8, pages 323–324

Materials   safety goggles
10 white foam balls
10 foam balls of another color
toothpicks

How does the nucleus of one atom differ from another? In this investigation, you will explore the makeup of the nucleus of different elements and different isotopes.

Procedure

1. Copy the data table below. Each column represents an atom.

Symbol	Number of Protons	Number of Neutrons	Atomic Number	Mass Number
$^4_2$He				
$^9_4$Be				
			5	11
	6			12
	7	7		
		8		15
		9	8	

2. Put on safety goggles.

3. Let the colored balls represent protons and the white balls represent neutrons. Assemble the helium nucleus represented by the symbol $^4_2$He. Then assemble the beryllium nucleus $^9_4$Be. Based on your models, fill in the missing data in the first two rows of your table.

4. Assemble a nucleus model for each of the five remaining rows in the table. To do this, first determine the missing numbers in each row. Then build the model. Use the periodic table to determine the identity of the element. Write the symbol using isotope notation.

Atoms and Isotopes, continued

Cleanup/Disposal

Return all materials and clean your work area. Wash your hands.

Analysis

1. How did you determine the numbers of protons and neutrons for the atom in the third row?

_____

2. How did you determine the number of neutrons in the fourth row?

_____

3. How did you determine the mass number in the fifth row?

_____

4. How did you determine the atomic number in the sixth row?

_____

5. How did you determine the mass number in the last row?

_____

Conclusions

1. Which two rows represent isotopes of the same element? What is the element?

_____

2. What does the bottom number in an isotope symbol mean?

_____

3. What does the mass number of an atom tell you?

_____

Explore Further

Construct nucleus models of other atoms, such as ^3_2He, ^6_3Li, ^7_3Li, $^{13}_6C$, $^{16}_8O$, $^{19}_9F$, and $^{19}_{10}Ne$. Use the models to quiz your classmates about atomic number, mass number, and the identity of an atom.

Isotopes of Centium

Use with Discovery Investigation 8, pages 329–330

Materials   safety goggles
pre-1982 pennies
post-1982 pennies
balance
plastic or paper cups

Most elements occur in nature as a mixture of two or more isotopes. Chlorine, for example, occurs as a mixture of 75.8% $^{35}_{17}$Cl and 24.2% $^{37}_{17}$Cl. As a result, chlorine has an average atomic mass of 35.5 amu. How can you determine average atomic mass? In this investigation, you will find out by using pennies to model two isotopes of an atom.

Procedure

1. Put on safety goggles. Obtain a mixture of "centium isotopes." Centium is an imaginary element with the symbol Cn. The pre-1982 pennies represent the isotope ^{A}Cn. The post-1982 pennies represent the isotope ^{B}Cn.

2. Determine the atomic mass of ^{A}Cn and the atomic mass of ^{B}Cn in grams. Then determine the average atomic mass of centium in grams. You can separate the two isotopes by date. Measuring the mass of one penny is not a good idea, however. Pennies may be worn in different ways, and any balance error will be significant.

Cleanup/Disposal

Return all materials and clean your work area. Wash your hands.

Isotopes of Centium, continued

Analysis

1. What is the atomic mass of isotope ^{A}Cn in grams?

_____

2. What is the atomic mass of isotope ^{B}Cn in grams?

_____

3. How did you determine these atomic masses?

_____

4. Based only on the mixture's total mass and the number of atoms in the mixture, what is the average mass of one atom?

_____

Conclusion

1. What is the percentage of each isotope in your mixture of centium?

_____

2. Based on these percentages, calculate the average atomic mass of centium. Use the atomic masses you already determined for each isotope.

_____

3. How does the average atomic mass you determined above compare with the average mass you determined in Analysis question 4? Explain any differences.

_____

_____

Explore Further

Copper consists of a mixture of 69.2% $^{63}_{29}$Cu (atomic mass $= 62.93$ amu) and 30.8% $^{65}_{29}$Cu (atomic mass $= 64.93$ amu). Calculate the average atomic mass of copper.

_____

_____

Express Lab 9
Use with Express Lab 9, page 341

Procedure

Most of the radiation you encounter daily is electromagnetic radiation. You can see visible light, but not other types of electromagnetic radiation. The table below lists the maximum energy of some types of electromagnetic radiation. Energy is given in units of joules. Use the table to answer the Analysis questions.

Analysis

1. Which electromagnetic radiation has the highest energy? Which has the lowest?

_____

_____

2. Some matter can be ionized by radiation energies as low as 6.63×10^{-19} joules. Which electromagnetic radiation can be ionizing? Which is always nonionizing? Explain your answers.

_____

_____

_____

Electromagnetic Radiation	Maximum Energy (joules)
radio waves	1.99×10^{-23}
visible light	4.97×10^{-19}
ultraviolet rays	3.32×10^{-18}
gamma rays	1.99×10^{-11}

Water That Glows

The colors you see around you are actually reflections of the visible light spectrum. They appear more distinct in bright room light than when the lights are dimmed. Some substances give off colors under other light sources, such as an ultraviolet lamp. Ultraviolet light is also called black light. Have you ever walked near black light and noticed how different your clothing appears?

Materials   safety goggles
              lab coat or apron
              tonic water
              600-mL beaker
              fluorescent or incandescent light source
              ultraviolet light source (black light)
              white piece of paper

Procedure

1. Put on safety goggles and a lab coat or apron.

2. Pour approximately 500 mL of tonic water into the beaker. Place it on the white piece of paper.

3. Observe the water under fluorescent or incandescent room lights. Record your observations in the data table below.

Light Source	Observations
fluorescent or incandescent light	
black light	

4. Turn off all the lights and completely darken the room. Turn on the black light and shine it on the water.

5. Record your observations.

Cleanup/Disposal

Pour the tonic water into a waste beaker. Return all materials. Clean your work area, and wash your hands.

Water That Glows, continued

Analysis

1. Describe the color and clarity of the tonic water in ordinary room light.

   _____

   _____

2. Describe the color and clarity of the tonic water in black light.

   _____

   _____

3. What other objects looked different in black light?

   _____

   _____

Conclusions

1. Ordinary room lights give off all the colors of the visible light spectrum. Black lights give off invisible ultraviolet light (and a little visible violet light). Explain why the tonic water looked colorless under normal room lights.

   _____

   _____

2. Tonic water contains a substance called quinine. It releases a certain wavelength and color of light. Why do you think the tonic water was the color you recorded in your table?

   _____

   _____

Explore Further

Have you ever used a "light stick"? Research their construction and the two substances they contain. Describe the chemical reaction that occurs in light sticks in terms of the electromagnetic spectrum and fluorescence.

_____

_____

Marshmallow Waves

Microwaves are nonionizing radiation on the electromagnetic spectrum. Microwave ovens cook unevenly because of a pattern of standing waves inside the chamber. If the food isn't rotated, hot spots develop. These spots can be used to measure the wavelength of the microwaves. Have you read the label on the back of a microwave oven? What information on the label is useful for calculating the speed of light?

Materials   safety goggles   paper plate
              lab coat or apron   toothpicks
              microwave oven   small bowl
              small marshmallows

Procedure

1. Put on safety goggles and a lab coat or apron.

2. Arrange marshmallows standing upright so they completely cover the paper plate.

3. If the microwave has a rotating plate inside, place a small bowl over the plate to prevent it from rotating. You do not want the plate of marshmallows to rotate or move while the oven is on.

4. Program the oven power to run at medium power. If the power is too high, the marshmallows puff up too fast.

5. Place the plate of marshmallows in the center of the oven. Turn the oven on. Time does not matter. Watch the marshmallows carefully. The marshmallows will puff up (or melt) at the hottest spots in the oven. In general, the marshmallows will be finished in 3 to 5 minutes. You do not want the marshmallow to burn. **Safety Alert: Never eat any substance used in an investigation.**

6. Open the door and remove the plate. Insert toothpicks into the marshmallow mounds with the greatest height. These represent wave crests. **Safety Alert: The marshmallows will be very hot when they come out of the oven.**

Marshmallow Waves, continued

7. Measure and record the distance, in centimeters, between two crests.

Cleanup/Disposal

Dispose of the marshmallows and plate in a waste container. Return all materials. Clean your work area, and wash your hands.

Analysis

1. What is the wavelength of the microwaves in centimeters?

_____

2. Calculate the speed of light, *c*, using the equation $c = \nu\lambda$
   Frequency, ν, is 2.450×10^9 Hertz or cycles/second. (The frequency can be found on the back of the microwave oven.) Wavelength, λ, is measured in centimeters per cycle. Express your answer in centimeters per second. _____

   Below is an example of how this calculation should be set up and solved.

   $$c = \left(\frac{2.450 \times 10^9 \ \cancel{cycles}}{second}\right)\left(\frac{wavelength\ from\ investigation\ cm}{\cancel{cycle}}\right)$$

Conclusions

1. The accepted value for the speed of light is 3.0×10^{10} cm/s. Calculate your percent error.

   Percent error is used to determine the accuracy of measurements when an accepted value is known. The formula for percent error is

   $$percent\ error = \left(\frac{difference\ between\ measured\ value\ and\ accepted\ value}{accepted\ value}\right) 100 \ \%$$

   What is your percent error? _____

Marshmallow Waves, continued

2. Compare your results with the results of classmates. List the
range of answers. Why do you think there is such a wide range
of answers?

_____

_____

_____

Explore Further

Are there microwave communication towers near your home or school?
Information can be transmitted by television, telephone, and radio waves.
Research how microwaves are used to transmit electronic information.

Modeling Radioactive Decay
Use with Investigation 9, pages 363–364

It is impossible to know when a particular radioactive nucleus will decay. However, it is possible to tell how many nuclei in a large sample will decay over time. How do radioactive nuclei decay over a certain number of half-lives? In this investigation, you will model radioactive decay.

Materials safety goggles
64 pennies
shoe box with lid

Procedure

1. Make a data table like the one below.

Number of Shakes	Pennies Removed	Pennies Remaining
0	0	64
1		
2		
3		

2. Put on safety goggles. Place the pennies in the shoe box and put the lid on the box. Shake the box for 5 seconds. **Safety Alert: Hold the lid firmly in place to keep the pennies inside the box.**

3. Remove the lid. Observe the pennies that are heads-up. Remove these pennies from the box. Count them and record this number. Then calculate and record the number of pennies remaining in the box.

4. Replace the lid on the box. Shake the box again for 5 seconds. Repeat step 3.

5. Continue shaking the box, removing heads-up pennies, and recording data until all pennies are removed from the box. Add rows to your data table as necessary.

Cleanup/Disposal

Return the materials. Then wash your hands.

Modeling Radioactive Decay, continued

Analysis

1. Graph your results. On the x axis, show the number of times the shoe box is shaken. on the y axis, show the number of pennies remaining after each shake. Connect your data points, making a smooth line.

2. How does the number of remaining pennies change with the number of shakes?

_____

3. What change in a radioactive substance does each shaking of the box represent? Explain your answer.

_____

_____

Conclusions

1. Based on your graph, how many shakes were required before 32 (or fewer) pennies remained? Before 16 (or fewer) remained? Before 4 (or fewer) remained?

_____

_____

2. Based on the definition of half-life, how many shakes should be required for just 1 penny to remain?

_____

3. How many shakes were actually required before you were left with 1 penny in your box?

_____

4. Do your answers for question 2 and 3 differ? If so, what might have caused the difference?

_____

_____

Explore Further

Repeat the procedure with a larger number of coins or other objects. Compare the new graph with the original one. Observe any change in your results.

Modeling Fission Chain Reactions
Use with Discovery Investigation 9, pages 373–374

When uranium-235 absorbs a neutron, 20 different fission reactions are possible. One such reaction is

$$^{235}U + {}_{0}^{1}n \rightarrow {}^{134}Xe + {}^{100}Sr + 2({}_{0}^{1}n)$$

Uranium fission reactions usually produce two or three neutrons, which go on to start other reactions. As more neutrons are produced, more reactions occur, producing even more neutrons. Too many reactions happening at once create an uncontrolled chain reaction. By removing some neutrons, the chain reaction can be controlled . How does removing neutrons affect a chain reaction? In this investigation, you will model a two-neutron reaction producing uncontrolled and controlled chain reactions.

Materials   70 dominoes

Procedure

1. Write a procedure for modeling a fission chain reaction in which each splitting nucleus produces two neutrons. Use dominoes for modeling the reaction.

2. Think of a way to model an uncontrolled reaction and then a controlled reaction. (Hint: An uncontrolled reaction might show many dominoes falling. A controlled reaction might show a limited number of dominoes falling.)

3. Have your procedure approved by your teacher. Then set up and try your model.

Cleanup/Disposal

Return the dominoes. Then wash your hands.

Modeling Fission Chain Reactions, continued

Analysis

1. How many dominoes fell over in the model of the uncontrolled reaction? How is this like an uncontrolled fission reaction?

_____

_____

2. How many dominoes fell over in the model of the controlled reaction? How is this like a controlled fission reaction?

_____

_____

Conclusions

1. Did your models accurately represent fission? Explain your answer.

_____

_____

2. How did your models of a controlled and uncontrolled reaction differ?

_____

_____

Explore Further

Think of another way to model fission reactions. Create your models. How do they compare to the domino models?

_____

_____

Express Lab 10

Use with Express Lab 10, page 387

Materials   safety goggles
different brands of wintergreen mints, broken in half
pliers
transparent tape

Procedure

1. Put on safety goggles.

2. Wrap each jaw of the pliers with tape.

3. Make the room as dark as possible.

4. Place a mint between the jaws of the pliers. Closely watch the broken edge of the mint as you crush it. Record your observations.

5. Repeat step 4 with the other mints.

Analysis

1. What did you observe when you crushed the mints?

_____

_____

2. How do you explain this observation?

_____

_____

Colored Flames and Electrons
Use with Investigation 10, pages 390–391

Sometimes laboratory instruments are required to identify an
element by its emission spectrum. However, some elements
produce colors you can see when their compounds are placed
in a flame. Are the results of such tests clear enough to identify
substances? In this investigation, you will use flame tests to identify
an unknown compound.

Materials   safety goggles
lab coat or apron
7 index cards
7 wood splints or wood-handled swabs
small sample of each compound listed in the data table
beaker
distilled water
Bunsen burner

Procedure

1. Make a data table like the one shown here. Then label each
index card with the name of a compound from the table.

Compound	Flame Color
lithium chloride	
potassium chloride	
sodium chloride	
strontium chloride	
calcium chloride	
barium chloride	
unknown	

2. Put on safety goggles and a lab coat or apron.

3. Obtain a small sample of each compound. Use the labeled
cards to carefully carry the samples to your work area.

Colored Flames and Electrons, continued

4. Pour some distilled water into the beaker. Place the 7 splints in the water. Light the burner. **Safety Alert: Be careful around an open flame. Tie back long hair and loose clothing. Never reach across a flame. Do not leave the flame unattended.**

5. Remove one splint from the water. Dip the tip of the soaked end into the sample of lithium chloride crystals.

6. Place the crystals into the burner flame. Observe and record the color of the flame. **Safety Alert: Do not hold the splint in the flame after observing the compound's flame color. Do not allow the wood to begin burning.**

7. Repeat steps 5 through 6 for each compound in the table, including the unknown.

Cleanup/Disposal

Return all equipment. Place the splints and unused samples in the proper waste containers. Clean your work area. Wash your hands.

Analysis

1. Why doesn't the chloride ion affect the color of the flame?

_____

2. How does the emission spectrum of an element relate to the colors produced?

_____

Conclusions

1. What is the identity of your unknown compound?

_____

2. Explain how you identified your unknown compound.

_____

Explore Further

Repeat the investigation using crystals of copper(II) chloride. What color is the copper flame?

_____

Emission Spectroscopy

According to the modern atomic model, electrons move about the nucleus within specific energy levels. If electrons absorb enough energy, they may leap to a higher level. When electrons return to their original level, a number of distinct energy emissions occur. Atoms of each element contain unique arrangements of electrons. The lines in their emission spectrum can be used as "spectral fingerprints." Have you wondered how astronomers know the chemical makeup of distant stars?

Materials   safety goggles
lab coat or apron
low-wattage incandescent lightbulb
fluorescent light source
high-voltage power supply for spectrum tubes
spectrum tubes (helium, hydrogen, mercury, and neon)
spectroscope

Procedure

1. Put on safety goggles and a lab coat or apron.

2. Use the spectroscope to observe the light emitted from a fluorescent light source. Record your observations in the data table by drawing a line corresponding to each wavelength shown in the spectrum.

3. Aim the spectroscope at the ordinary lightbulb. Record your observations in the table by drawing the lines shown in the spectrum.

4. Your teacher will operate the four spectrum tubes. Once the power supply is turned on, aim the spectroscope at the glowing tube. For each tube, record the position of each bright emission line in the data table on the next page.

Emission Spectroscopy, continued

Light Source	Wavelength (nm) of Emission Spectrum Lines			
	400	**500**	**600**	**700**
fluorescent light				
incandescent light				
He gas tube				
H gas tube				
Hg gas tube				
Ne gas tube				

Cleanup/Disposal

Return all materials. Clean your work area and wash your hands.

Analysis

1. Compare the spectra for incandescent and fluorescent light. How are they different? _____

   _____

2. Name one way electrons were excited in this investigation.

   _____

Conclusions

1. Why does each element in the gas tubes emit a unique line spectrum? _____

   _____

2. Before its discovery on Earth, helium's existence was first observed in the sun. Explain how this was possible. _____

   _____

Explore Further

Conduct flame tests on several elements. Use the spectroscope to record each emission spectrum. Compare the wavelengths to the colors seen with the naked eye.

Electron Configurations of Atoms and Ions

Chemical properties are related to the arrangement of electrons. An electron configuration shows the energy levels (1, 2, etc.) and orbitals (*s, p, d, f*) of the electrons in an atom or ion. The colors of solutions containing metal ions are related to their filled orbitals. Filled orbitals often present no color. Partially filled orbitals, especially *d* orbitals, usually result in a color. Look at the metals in the periodic table. Which ones do you think will result in colored solutions?

Materials   safety goggles
lab coat or apron
well plate
eyedroppers for delivering drops of each solution below
1.0 M NaCl
0.1 M FeCl$_3$
0.2 M CuSO$_4$
0.2 M ZnCl$_2$
0.05 M AgNO$_3$
0.2 M NiSO4
0.5 M CaCl$_2$
0.2 M MgSO$_4$
0.2 M AlCl$_3$
0.5 M NaOH

Procedure

1. Put on safety goggles and a lab coat or apron.

2. Half-fill a well in the well plate with each solution listed at the top of the data table below. You should fill nine wells in the order the solutions are listed. Observe each solution and record its color in the first row of the table.

Well	NaCl	FeCl$_3$	CuSO$_4$	ZnCl$_2$	AgNO$_3$	NiSO$_4$	CaCl$_2$	MgSO$_4$	AlCl$_3$
before adding NaOH									
after adding NaOH									

Electron Configurations of Atoms and Ions, continued

3. Add 5 drops of 0.5 M NaOH to each half-filled well. Use free, hanging drops. Do not dip the dropper tip into the solutions since this contaminates them.

4. Observe and record any changes in the second row of the table.

Cleanup/Disposal

Rinse your well plate with a large amount of water. Return all materials. Clean your work area, and wash your hands.

Analysis

1. Write the electron configurations for sodium, magnesium, and aluminum.

_____

_____

_____

2. Metals form ions when they lose valence electrons. Write the electron configurations for sodium, magnesium, and aluminum cations.

_____

_____

3. Nonmetals form ions when they gain valence electrons. Write the electron configuration for the chloride ion.

_____

4. Transition metal ions having partially filled d orbitals usually have color. Which solutions contain transition metal ions with this characteristic?

_____

_____

Electron Configurations of Atoms and Ions, continued

5. Transition metals usually lose *s* orbital electrons first. Write the electron configurations for the following atoms and ions: Fe, Fe^{3+}, Ni, and Ni^{2+}.

_____

_____

_____

_____

6. Solutions containing silver and zinc cations have no color. What does this suggest about their electron configurations?

_____

_____

Conclusions

1. Write a general statement about which ions produced color, and why.

_____

_____

2. Predict which of the following transition metal cations have color: Cr^{3+}, Cd^{2+}, Hg^{2+}, and V^{2+}.

_____

_____

3. Predict which solutions would produce a color if mixed with sodium carbonate, Na_2CO_3.

_____

_____

Explore Further

Copper and silver have electron configurations that cannot be predicted. Use the Internet to research copper and silver's configurations. Why are copper and silver different?

_____

Valence Electrons of Metals

Use with Discovery Investigation 10, pages 397–398

The number of valence electrons in an atom helps determine how the atom reacts with other atoms. In this investigation, you will use an acid and a metal to produce hydrogen gas. How do the volumes of hydrogen gas compare for two different metals? How does each volume relate to the number of valence electrons in the metal?

Materials safety goggles
           lab coat or apron
           0.10 g of magnesium ribbon
           0.11 g of aluminum foil
           balance
           2 Erlenmeyer flasks
           2 1-hole stoppers that fit the flasks
           2 pieces of glass or hard plastic tubing
           2 pieces of flexible plastic or rubber tubing, each about 0.5 m
           2 250-mL beakers
           2 water troughs or plastic basins
           20 mL of 3 *M* hydrochloric acid
           10-mL graduated cylinder

Procedure

1. Write a procedure describing how you will react excess hydrochloric acid (10 mL) with metal in a flask and collect the hydrogen gas produced. (Hint: You can collect gas by bubbling it into an upside-down beaker filled with water.) You will follow the procedure twice, once for each metal. Include a hypothesis and the following safety alerts in your procedure. **Safety Alerts: Take care with glassware. Hydrogen gas burns; do not have open flames in the lab. Report any acid spills to your teacher immediately.**

2. Have your teacher approve your procedure.

3. Put on safety goggles and a lab coat or apron. Follow your procedure using magnesium, then aluminum.

Valence Electrons of Metals, continued

4. For each metal, estimate the volume of hydrogen gas produced. Find a simple, whole-number ratio that relates the two volumes.

Cleanup/Disposal

Dispose of the reaction products properly. Clean and dry the glassware. Return all equipment. Clean your work area, and wash your hands.

Analysis

1. Write a balanced chemical equation for each reaction that took place.

_____

_____

_____

2. From these equations, how many moles of hydrogen can be produced from 1 mol of each metal?

_____

3. Use your answer to question 2 to predict the smallest whole-number ratio of the two volumes of hydrogen produced.

_____

Conclusions

1. How did your experimental ratio (from Procedure step 4) compare to your predicted ratio (from Analysis question 3)?

_____

_____

Valence Electrons of Metals, continued

2. Locate magnesium and aluminum on the periodic table. How many valence electrons does each atom have? Compare the ratio of hydrogen volumes to the ratio of valence electrons.

_____

_____

Explore Further

Use the periodic table to find the number of valence electrons in a sodium atom. Predict the ratio of volumes of hydrogen produced if sodium and magnesium were the metals used in this investigation.

Express Lab 11
Use with Express Lab 11, page 426

Procedure

Mendeleev predicted the properties of the element between calcium and titanium. This element was unknown at the time. He used properties of nearby elements to do this. Use the information in the table to predict the properties of this element.

Analysis

1. What is a likely density for the unknown element?

_____

2. What is its likely atomic mass?

_____

3. How many valence electrons might the unknown element have? Explain how you obtained your answer.

_____

_____

_____

Element	Atomic Mass (amu)	Density (g/cm³)	Chlorine Compound
potassium	39.1	0.86	KCl
calcium	40.1	1.55	$CaCl_2$
unknown element			
titanium	47.9	4.51	$TiCl_4$

Periodic Change in Atomic Radius
Use with Investigation 11, pages 438–439

Materials   compass
pencil
metric ruler (showing millimeters)
worksheet

Atomic radius differs with each element. How does atomic radius change across a period? How does it vary between periods? In this investigation, you will model data to show these changes.

Procedure

1. Look at the table on the next page. It lists the atomic radius for 21 elements in periods 2, 3, and 4. You will model the size of these atoms by drawing circles to represent them. The radius for each circle is listed under "Model Radius." For example, lithium's atomic radius is 157 pm. The radius of the circle representing this atom will be 16 mm.

2. Use the ruler and compass to draw your models in the table on the worksheet. Start with lithium. In the upper left square, draw a circle with a radius of 16 mm (a diameter of 32 mm). Write *Li* inside the circle. **Safety Alert: The compass has a very sharp point. Handle the compass with care.**

3. Complete the worksheet by repeating step 2 for each element listed. Label each model with its chemical symbol.

4. Check that the order of your models reflects the order of elements in periods 2, 3, and 4 of the periodic table. The noble gases are not modeled.

Cleanup/Disposal

Return all materials.

Chemistry

Periodic Change in Atomic Radius, continued

Analysis

1. What is the relationship between atomic radius and the corresponding model radius?

_____

_____

2. Some atoms are nearly the same size. Do your models demonstrate small size differences? Explain.

_____

_____

Conclusions

1. How does atomic radius change from left to right across a period?

_____

_____

2. How does atomic radius change for elements in a column as the period number increases?

_____

_____

3. Why does the radius increase at the beginning of each new period?

_____

_____

Periodic Change in Atomic Radius, continued

Explore Further

Discuss other methods of modeling the pattern of atomic size in the periodic table. Using one of these methods, model the atomic radius data provided in this investigation. Compare the two modeling methods.

Element	Period	Atomic Radius (pm)	Model Radius (mm)
Li	2	157	16
Be	2	112	11
B	2	88	9
C	2	77	8
N	2	74	7
O	2	66	7
F	2	64	6
Na	3	191	19
Mg	3	160	16
Al	3	143	14
Si	3	118	12
P	3	110	11
S	3	104	10
Cl	3	99	10
K	4	235	23
Ca	4	197	20
Ga	4	153	15
Ge	4	122	12
As	4	121	12
Se	4	117	12
Br	4	114	11

Modeling a Pattern in the Periodic Table

Periodic patterns are sometimes difficult to visualize. A model can help you see the patterns across periods and down columns of the periodic table. How could you model a pattern in the periodic table using drinking straws?

Materials   safety goggles
                    lab coat or apron
                    small cardboard box top (or well plate with at least 48 small
                        wells that fit drinking straws)
                    drinking straws
                    paper for cutting out 48 round labels, each 1 cm in diameter
                    tape or glue
                    scissors
                    charts of periodic properties (atomic radius, ionic radius,
                        ionization energy, electron affinity, and electronegativity)
                    string

Procedure

1. Put on safety goggles and a lab coat or apron.

2. Select one of the periodic properties charts. You will create a model of this periodic property by using varying lengths of drinking straws. Use the data for the representative elements (columns 1, 2, and 13–18). Do not model the transition metals (columns 3–12).

3. Sketch columns 1, 2, and 13–18 of the periodic table onto the box top, making a square for each representative element. In the middle of each square, make a 1-cm hole. Do not place your holes too close together. If you are using a well plate, omit this step.

4. Cut out 48 round labels, each 1 cm in diameter. On each label, write the element symbol and the value of the periodic property you selected.

Modeling a Pattern in the Periodic Table, continued

5. For each element, cut a piece of straw. Base the straw length on the appropriate conversion below. Add an extra 1.5 cm of length to each straw. This is for insertion into the box top (or well plate).

6. Assemble your model to represent the periodic property you selected. Make sure each straw length is in the correct hole and is labeled correctly.

Periodic Property	Measurement Conversion for Model
atomic radius	50 pm = 1 cm in model
ionic radius	30 pm = 1 cm in model
ionization energy	500 kJ = 1 cm in model
electron affinity	500 kJ = 1 cm in model
electronegativity	1 unit = 1 cm in model

Cleanup/Disposal

Return all materials. Clean your work area and wash your hands.

Analysis

1. As you move across a period, what general pattern do you see?

_____

_____

2. As you move down a column, what general pattern do you see?

_____

_____

3. Use the string to mark the staircase dividing metals and nonmetals. Do you see any differences in the periodic property values as you cross this line?

_____

_____

Modeling a Pattern in the Periodic Table, continued

Conclusions

How effective was your model at helping you visualize a periodic pattern? What are some of the strengths and weaknesses of your model?

_____

_____

Explore Further

Many teachers use models to explain concepts. Interview several teachers. Ask them to describe or show you three different models they use. As a class, make a list of these models. Discuss the benefits and any misunderstandings that might occur in using these models.

_____

_____

_____

Ionization Energy

Use with Discovery Investigation 11, pages 445–446

Materials graph paper
     red, blue, and green pens

The number of valence electrons and protons in an atom affect ionization energy. How does ionization energy change across a period and within a family? In this investigation, you will make a graph to show how ionization energy changes.

Procedure

1. Write a hypothesis predicting how ionization energy varies within a period and within a family.

_____

2. Write a procedure that tells how to graph the data in the table on the next page . The graph should show how ionization energy changes across a period and within a family. Plot all of the data on one graph. Use a different colored pen for each period.

_____

_____

_____

Ionization Energy, continued

Element	Valence Electrons	Ionization Energy (kJ/mol)	Element	Valence Electrons	Ionization Energy (kJ/mol)
Li	1	520	P	5	1,012
Be	2	899	S	6	1,000
B	3	801	Cl	7	1,251
C	4	1,086	Ar	8	1,520
N	5	1,402	K	1	419
O	6	1,314	Ca	2	590
F	7	1,681	Ga	3	579
Ne	8	2,081	Ge	4	762
Na	1	496	As	5	947
Mg	2	738	Se	6	941
Al	3	578	Br	7	1,140
Si	4	786	Kr	8	1,351

3. Have your hypothesis and procedure approved by your teacher. Then construct your graph.

Cleanup/Disposal

Return any materials.

Analysis

1. Describe how you graphed the data. What units did you choose for the *x* axis and *y* axis? Explain your choices.

_____

_____

2. Does your graph show a steady change in ionization energy in a given period? If not, which elements do not follow the pattern?

_____

_____

Ionization Energy, continued

3. Describe how ionization energy within a family changes as
the period number increases. Explain this pattern in terms of
atomic structure.

_____

_____

Conclusions

1. You graphed data for three periods. In each period, what
element has the lowest ionization energy? Explain why these
elements are easy to ionize.

_____

_____

2. Why do noble gases require so much energy to be ionized?

_____

3. Why do you think alkaline earth metals have higher ionization
energies than elements in the boron family?

_____

Explore Further

Use reference books or the Internet to find ionization energies for
the representative elements in period 5. Add these elements to your
graph. Compare the trend you see in period 5 with the trends in
periods 2, 3, and 4.

_____

_____

Comparing Properties in a Family

You have read about the reactivity of various elements. Many metals are unstable in their pure form. Some will even explode if exposed to moist air. Reactivity depends on valence electrons. The property of being relatively unreactive is important in many applications involving metals. Certain metals are used in jewelry making. Can you imagine if your rings dissolved while washing dishes?

Materials safety goggles   small pieces of the following elements:
       lab coat or apron   magnesium
       well plate   aluminum
       600-mL beaker   sulfur
       wash bottle   iron
       soap   nickel
       6 *M* HCl in pipets   copper
                  zinc
                  carbon
                  silicon (2 pieces)
                  tin
                  lead

Procedure

 1. Put on safety goggles and a lab coat or apron.

Comparing Properties in a Family, continued

2. Place one small piece of each element into a well in the well plate, according to the data table below.

Al	Al	Si	Si
Fe	Ni	Cu	Zn
C	Si	Sn	Pb

3. Using the pipet of HCl, quickly half-fill the wells in the first row.

4. Record your observations in the table.

5. Repeat steps 3 and 4 for row 2. Record your observations.

6. Repeat steps 3 and 4 for row 3. Record your observations.

Cleanup/Disposal

Wash the well plate using plenty of water. Return all materials. Clean your work area, and wash your hands.

Comparing Properties in a Family, continued

Analysis

1. Rank the elements shown in row 1 of the data table in order of reactivity (from high to low).

_____

2. Rank the elements shown in row 2 of the data table in order of reactivity (from high to low).

_____

3. Rank the elements shown in row 3 of the data table in order of reactivity (from high to low).

_____

Conclusions

1. Compare each element's rank with its location in the periodic table. For each element, record its family name and the number of valence electrons.

_____

_____

2. Predict the properties of strontium, silver, and antimony. Rank them in order of reactivity based on your conclusions above.

_____

_____

Explore Further

Electrical wiring is typically made of copper strands covered with insulation. Although relatively inexpensive, copper is not always the best choice for electrical conductivity. Investigate which metals are the best conductors. Relate this to the cost of some electronics, such as computers.

_____

_____

Express Lab 12

Use with Express Lab 12, page 467

Materials   water faucet
             plastic comb

Procedure

1. Turn on the faucet so that a small stream of water flows.

2. Comb your hair with the plastic comb for 10 seconds.

3. Move the comb so that it is near, but not touching, the stream of water.

Analysis

1. Record your observations.

   _____

   _____

2. What type of bonding must be present in a water molecule? Explain your answer.

   _____

   _____

   _____

Chromatography and Polarity
Use with Investigation 12, pages 490–491

Materials   safety goggles   pencil
                      lab coat or apron   metric ruler
                      600-mL beaker or other container   3 toothpicks
                      isopropyl alcohol-water solution   red, blue, and green food dyes
                      scissors   tape
                      chromatography paper   clear plastic wrap

Chromatography is a method used to separate the substances in a mixture. Each substance is carried by a solvent at a different speed. This speed is based on how much attraction the substance has for the paper and for the solvent. A polar solvent attracts polar substances in a mixture more than nonpolar substances. How is separation by chromatography related to polarity? You will find out in this investigation.

Procedure

1. Put on safety goggles and a lab coat or apron.

2. Add the alcohol-water solution to the beaker until it is about 1 cm deep.

3. Cut three identical strips of paper. The three strips must be able to fit in the beaker as shown. Draw a pencil line 1 cm from the end of each paper strip. Using the toothpicks, center a spot of food dye on each line. Use a different color of dye for each strip.

4. Tape the strips to the pencil as shown, and place the pencil on top of the beaker. The ends of the strips must be barely in the solution. Cover the top of the beaker with clear plastic wrap to reduce evaporation.

5. Wait about 25 minutes while the solution moves up the paper. Then remove the strips from the solution. Allow them to dry overnight.

Chromatography and Polarity, continued

6. The next day, make a data table like the one below. Record in your table the colors that are in each dye. Also measure and record how far each color traveled up the paper.

Dye Color	Colors of Substances in Dye	Distance Traveled from Line (cm)
red		
blue		
green		

Cleanup/Disposal

Pour the solution down the drain with running water. Wash the beaker and return all equipment. Clean your work area and wash your hands.

Analysis

1. Which substance in each dye traveled farthest?

_____

2. Which substance in each dye traveled the least distance?

_____

Conclusions

1. Which substance in each dye is likely to contain polar molecules?

_____

2. Which substance in each dye is likely to contain molecules with little or no polarity?

_____

Explore Further

Repeat the investigation using pure water as the solvent. Compare your results to those using the alcohol-water solution.

_____

_____

Swirling Hydrogen Bonds

Hydrogen bonding affects viscosity, or the ability of a fluid to pour or flow. Liquids with strong hydrogen bonds tend to form bulging drops, appear thicker, and are less able to flow. Hydrogen bonding also affects surface tension, or the ability of a liquid to behave as if it were covered by a thin skin. Objects also tend to stand on the surfaces of the liquids longer. This is the reason a water bug can walk on water and a straight pin will lay on the surface of water. The stronger the hydrogen bonding, the more the particles pull together. Can you actually see the effects of different strengths of hydrogen bonding? In this investigation, you will find out.

Materials   safety goggles
lab coat or apron
four 300-mL Erlenmeyer or Florence flasks
four stoppers to fit flasks
masking tape
four 100-mL graduated cylinders
glycerin
ethylene glycol
ethanol
distilled water
stopwatch or timer

Procedure

1. Put on safety goggles and a lab coat or apron.

2. Obtain four flasks. Use the tape and a pen to label each flask with one of the four liquids listed in the data table.

3. Fill each flask with 100 mL of the liquid on the label. Stopper each flask. **Safety Alert: Handle glass with care. Report any broken or chipped glass to your teacher immediately. Wipe up all spills immediately. Some chemicals are toxic. Do not get chemical on your skin or in your mouth. If this happens, report immediately.**

4. Gently rotate the flask containing glycerin **10 times** so that the fluid contents form a swirling vortex.

Swirling Hydrogen Bonds, continued

5. Once you have created a steady vortex, carefully put the flask
   down. Observe how long it takes the vortex to disappear after
   you stop rotating the flask. Record the time in seconds for
   Trial 1.

	Time for Vortex to Stop Swirling (sec)			
Liquid	Trial 1	Trial 2	Trial 3	Average time
glycerin				
ethylene glycol				
ethanol				
distilled water				

6. Repeat steps 4 and 5 for the next three liquids. Be sure to rotate
   the flasks in the same manner each time.

7. Complete the next two trials by repeating steps 4 and 5.

8. Calculate the average time for each liquid and record the
   information in the data table.

Cleanup/Disposal

Return the fluids to the correct containers. Wash the glassware, and
return all materials. Clean your work area, and wash your hands.

Analysis

1. Why was it important to repeat the same swirling procedure
   for each liquid?

   _____

2. Rank the fluids' increased strength to decreased strength of the
   hydrogen bonds.

   _____

Swirling Hydrogen Bonds, continued

Conclusions

1. How does hydrogen bonding affect the swirling of fluids?

_____

_____

2. Based upon your answer in #1, what predictions can you make about its molecular shape?

_____

_____

Explore Further

Research and draw the structural formulas for each compound. Indicate the areas of the hydrogen bonding on your drawing.

Alchemist's Dream: Creating an Alloy

Alchemy was practiced in China and India as early as 400 B.C. The goal was to change common metals into gold. Although unsuccessful in this, they spurred the development of science. They discovered chemicals, designed laboratory apparatus, and developed many procedures. Mimicking precious metals, alchemists actually created silver and gold "brass." Why do you think people would bite their gold and silver coins?

Materials
safety goggles
lab coat or apron
3 clean pennies
ring stand
test tube clamp
ring clamp
large glass funnel
tubing
sink faucet with suction sidearm
large evaporation dish
large watch glass

Bunsen burner
striker
medium beaker
4 *M* NaOH
small graduated cylinder
zinc dust
scoopula
crucible tongs
conductivity device

Procedure

1. Put on safety goggles and a lab coat or apron.

2. Set up your mini fume hood. Clamp a glass funnel, upside down, at the top of your ring stand. Connect tubing from the funnel stem to the suction arm of the sink faucet. Arrange a ring clamp below the funnel to hold the large evaporation dish. Position the Bunsen burner below the ring clamp. **Safety Alert: Handle glass with care. Report any broken or chipped glass to your teacher immediately. Wipe up all spills immediately.**

3. Record the appearance of the untreated pennies in the data table.

Alchemist's Dream: Creating an Alloy, continued

Observations	Untreated	Treated with Zn	Treated with Zn and heated in flame
appearance of penny			
conductivity test			

4. Into an evaporation dish, place a small scoopula of zinc dust (~0.5 g) and 15 mL of a sodium hydroxide solution. **Safety Alert: Some chemicals are toxic. Do not get chemical on your skin or in your mouth. If this happens, report it immediately. Sodium hydroxide is very caustic to the skin and nasal passages. Avoid fumes produced.**

5. Place the dish of sodium hydroxide and zinc on the ring of the ring stand. Make sure it is secure and will not tip over. Place the watch glass on the evaporation dish. Position the funnel over the dish. Start the mini fume hood at your lab station by turning on the sink water.

6. Light your Bunsen burner. Adjust it to produce a small flame. Heat the solution gently until it just begins to bubble. **Safety Alert: Use care around hot objects. Report any burns immediately.** Do not allow the solution to boil. Avoid the vapors.

7. Using crucible tongs, carefully place two pennies into the hot solution. Cover with the watchglass. The third penny is used as a control.

8. Allow the pennies to react in the solution. You should notice them start to turn a gray-silver color. In the meanwhile, fill a beaker with tap water.

9. When the pennies appear coated with zinc dust, move the Bunsen burner aside. Use tongs to remove the pennies and place them in the beaker of water. Gently rub off any excess zinc. If stubborn, use the test tube brush to gently scrub. Do not use a paper towel to remove the zinc. Record your observations in the data table.

10. Rinse the beaker and refill with tap water.

Alchemist's Dream: Creating an Alloy, continued

11. Choose one of the treated pennies and hold it with the crucible tongs. Heat it in the burner flame. Watch carefully for a color change. As soon as it appears, quickly drop the penny into the water. Turn off the burner.

12. Remove the penny from the water and dry gently. Compare to the other two pennies. Record your observations in your data table

13. Test each of the three pennies with a conductivity device. Record your observations for each penny.

Cleanup/Disposal

Place the evaporating dish of sodium hydroxide and zinc in the main fume hood. Your instructor will neutralize and dispose of it. Wash the glassware, and return all materials. Clean your work area, and wash your hands.

Analysis

Compare the treated pennies to the untreated one. How closely do the treated pennies resemble other, more precious, metals?

_____

_____

Conclusions

What practical uses (business, industry, fashion, etc.) might there be for the procedure that seemed to turn your pennies into gold and silver?

_____

_____

Explore Further

The blending of copper and zinc creates white brass. The heating of this metal causes a color change to yellow brass. Research and write a lab activity to create and bronze another copper alloy.

_____

_____

_____

Forces Between Molecules

Use with Discovery Investigation 12, pages 499–500

Materials   safety goggles
                lab coat or apron
                candle and holder
                matches
                400-mL beaker
                beaker tongs
                4 ice cubes
                strip of cobalt chloride
                paper

The properties of a molecular compound are affected by the attractive forces between its molecules. What can you conclude about these forces by observing the properties of the compound? In this investigation, you will examine a property of carbon dioxide and water vapor. These gases are formed by combustion.

Procedure

1. Using the materials provided, write a procedure to compare how easily CO_2 and H_2O change from a gas to a liquid. Both gases are produced by a burning candle. Include a hypothesis and safety alerts in your procedure. Cobalt chloride paper is used to detect the presence of liquid water.

2. Make a table to record your observations.

3. After your teacher approves your procedure, perform the investigation.

Forces Between Molecules, continued

Cleanup/Disposal

Return the equipment and properly dispose of materials. Clean your work area and wash your hands.

Analysis

1. What did you observe when you cooled the gaseous products of the burning candle?

_____

_____

2. What did you learn by using the cobalt chloride paper?

_____

_____

3. Water boils at 100°C, while carbon dioxide is a gas at temperatures above −78°C. Use this information to explain your answers to questions 1 and 2.

_____

_____

_____

Conclusions

1. What type of bond is present in a water molecule? In a carbon dioxide molecule?

_____

_____

2. Use dot diagrams to determine if the molecules of each substance are polar.

_____

_____

Forces Between Molecules, continued

3. Based on your answers to questions 1 and 2, list the
interparticle forces acting on each substance.

_____

_____

_____

4. How do your answers to questions 1–3 help explain
your results?

_____

_____

_____

Explore Further

Dihydrogen sulfide, H_2S, is a poisonous gas with a boiling point
of $-60°C$. Draw a dot diagram for H_2S and determine its geometry.
Form a hypothesis explaining why H_2S boils at a much lower
temperature than H_2O.

Determining the Specific Heat of Metals
Use with Investigation 13, page 517–518

In a closed system, the heat absorbed by one substance equals the heat released by another. Can you identify a substance from its specific heat? In this investigation, you will determine the specific heat for two known metals and one unknown metal.

Materials
safety goggles
lab coat or apron
2 foam cups
balance
100-mL graduated cylinder
water
stirring rod
2 thermometers
400-mL beaker
hot plate
large test tube
2 known metal samples
unknown metal sample
ring stand
test-tube clamp
tongs

Procedure

1. On a sheet of paper, make three tables like the one below, one for each metal sample.

Sample: _____	Data
mass of empty calorimeter	
mass of calorimeter and water	
mass of empty test tube	
mass of test tube and metal	
initial metal temperature	
initial water temperature	
final temperature	

Determining the Specific Heat of Metals, continued

2. Put on safety goggles and a lab coat or apron. Make a calorimeter by placing one foam cup inside another. Measure and record its mass.

3. Measure about 80 mL of water and pour this into the calorimeter. Measure and record the mass of the calorimeter and water. Place the stirring rod and one thermometer in the calorimeter.

4. Pour about 300 mL of water into the 400-mL beaker. Place this on a hot plate. Turn on the hot plate. Bring the water to a boil. **Safety Alert: Be careful when working near a hot plate.**

5. Measure and record the mass of the large test tube. Place pieces of one known metal into it until it is half full. Measure and record the mass of the tube and contents.

6. Support the test tube in the boiling water as shown. Heat the tube in boiling water for about 10 minutes. Turn off the hot plate. Measure the temperature of the boiling water. Record this as the initial temperature of the metal.

7. Stir the water in the calorimeter and measure its temperature. Record this as the initial temperature of the water.

8. Quickly transfer the metal from the test tube to the calorimeter without splashing. **Safety Alert: Be careful not to touch the water or the metal.** Stir the contents of the calorimeter for about 20 seconds. Record the final temperature of the water and metal (same temperature). Empty the calorimeter, saving the metal.

9. Repeat steps 3–8 for the other known metal and then for the unknown.

Cleanup/Disposal

Turn off the hot plate. Cool the water and then discard it, saving the metal samples. Dry and return the samples. Return all equipment. Wash your hands.

Determining the Specific Heat of Metals, continued

Analysis

1. Calculate the specific heat of each known metal.

_____

2. What assumption is made about the initial temperature of the metal and the calorimeter?

_____

3. Calculate the specific heat of the unknown metal.

_____

Conclusions

1. Compare your calculated values for the known samples with the accepted specific heat of each metal.

_____

_____

2. What is the identity of your unknown metal?

_____

_____

3. Identify and explain possible sources of error in this experiment.

_____

_____

Explore Further

Suggest a way to determine the specific heat of a liquid substance.

_____

_____

Express Lab 13

Use with Express Lab 13, page 521

Materials   safety goggles
lab coat or apron
25–30 g of iron powder
1 g of NaCl (sodium chloride)
plastic, self-sealing bag
1 large spoonful of vermiculite
5 mL of water

Procedure

1. Put on safety goggles and a lab coat or apron.

2. Place 25 to 30 g of iron powder into the plastic bag. Add 1 g of NaCl.

3. Seal the bag and shake to mix the contents.

4. Open the bag and add the vermiculite. Seal the bag and shake again to mix the contents.

5. Open the bag and add the water. Seal the bag and shake or squeeze it to mix the contents.

6. Wait about 1 minute. Record any observations.

Analysis

1. What did you observe after step 6?

_____

2. How can you explain this observation?

_____

_____

Heat of Reaction: Hot Packs and Cold Packs

Hot packs are made with a capsule of one chemical inside a bag of water. When you break the capsule, the substance mixes with the water. Energy is released during the separation of bonds and the surrounding water heats up. Cold packs contain capsules with chemicals that absorb energy from the water. This causes a decrease in the water temperature. How do manufacturers decide upon the best chemicals for these packs?

Materials   safety goggles
          lab coat or apron
          large test tube (20 mL or larger)
          test tube rack
          10-mL graduated cylinder
          thermometer
          $CaCl_2$
          NH_4NO_3
          NaOH
          KNO_3
          KCl
          digital balance
          weighing paper
          stopwatch or timer
          chemical supply catalog

Procedure

1. Put on safety goggles and a lab coat or apron.

2. Place 10 mL of distilled water into the test tube. Insert a thermometer. After one minute, record the water temperature under beginning temperature. **Safety Alert: Handle glass with care. Report any broken or chipped glass to your teacher immediately. Wipe up all spills immediately.**

Heat of Reaction: Hot Packs and Cold Packs, continued

Compound	Mass (g)	Beginning Water Temperature without Compound (°C)	Greatest Temperature Difference with Compound (°C)	Increase in Temperature	Decrease in Temperature
$CaCl_2$					
NH_4NO_3					
NaOH					
KNO_3					

3. Place a piece of weighing paper on the balance. Press the tare button. The display should read 0.00. The balance will ignore the mass of the weighing paper. Do not remove the paper. Measure and record the mass of approximately 1.0 g of $CaCl_2$. **Safety Alert: Digital balances are extremely accurate and sensitive measuring devices. Do not press on the pan. Avoid spilling on it. Some chemicals are toxic. Do not get chemical on your skin or in your mouth. If this happens, report it immediately.**

4. Carefully add the $CaCl_2$ to the test tube. Place the thermometer in the test tube. Watch for the greatest temperature change, hot or cold. Record the greatest difference in the chart. Be sure to check the correct box to indicate if the temperature increased or decreased.

5. Pour the contents of the test tube down the drain with the water running. Clean the test tube and thermometer.

6. Repeat steps 2 through 5 for the remaining three substances.

Cleanup/Disposal

Wash the glassware, and return all materials. Clean your work area, and wash your hands.

Heat of Reaction: Hot Packs and Cold Packs, continued

Analysis

1. Rank the four substances from most exothermic to most endothermic. Beside each, label their ΔT. Be sure to indicate if this is a "$+$" or "$-$" temperature change.

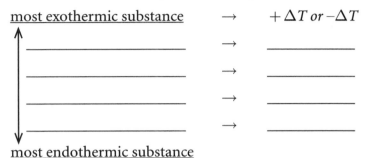

most exothermic substance $\quad \rightarrow \quad +\Delta T \ or \ -\Delta T$

most endothermic substance

2. Use a chemical supply catalog and look up the cost per gram for each substance. Record the cost of 1.0 g of each chemical.

_____

_____

Conclusions

1. Based upon temperature change and cost per gram, which substance would make the best hot pack? _____

2. Based upon temperature change and cost per gram, which substance would make the best cold pack? _____

Explore Further

At a local athletic supply store, record the ingredients of hot and cold packs. Did you see any substances listed that were used in this investigation? What other factors need to be considered when making these packs?

_____

_____

_____

Heat of Combustion: Candle Wax

One type of heat of reaction is heat of combustion. Many combustion reactions involve a substance with hydrogen and carbon changing into carbon dioxide and water. Energy is stored in the bonds between carbons, and carbon-hydrogen bonds. In the case of a burning candle, energy is released as heat and light. During a candle's combustion, is the wick burning or the wax?

Materials   safety goggles
lab coat or apron
candle
aluminum foil
matches
electronic balance
calculator

Procedure

1. Put on safety goggles and a lab coat or apron.

2. Place the candle on a small piece of aluminum foil on a balance.

3. Record the mass of the foil and candle before burning. **Safety Alert: Digital balances are extremely accurate and sensitive measuring devices. Do not press on the pan. Avoid spilling on it.**

Candle	Before burning (step 3)	After burning (step 6)
mass (g)		

4. Place the candle and foil on the lab table. **Safety Alert: Use care around hot objects. Report any burns immediately.**

5. Let the candle burn for 5 minutes.

6. After 5 minutes, extinguish the flame.

7. Measure and record the mass of the candle and foil system after burning.

Heat of Combustion: Candle Wax, continued

Cleanup/Disposal

Return all materials. Clean your work area, and wash your hands.

Analysis

1. The formula for candle wax can be approximated as C_2OH_{42}. Write the balanced chemical equation for the combustion of candle wax.

   _____

2. What is the difference between the candle before burning and after? _____

3. Calculate the moles of candle wax burned in the experiment.

   _____

4. Use the formula and standards below to calculate the heat of combustion of candle wax.

   (a) The heat of reaction, ΔH_{rxn}, of the reactant, candle wax $=-2{,}230$ kJ/mol. Use the balanced chemical equation from #1 and multiply the mol C_2OH_{42} by $-2{,}230$ kJ/mol.

   _____

   (b) The heat of reaction, ΔH_{rxn}, of the product, carbon dioxide $=-394$ kJ/mol. Use the balanced chemical equation from #1 and multiply the moles of carbon dioxide by -394 kJ/mol.

   _____

   (c) The heat of reaction, ΔH_{rxn}, of the product, water $=$ -242 kJ/mol. Use the balanced chemical equation from #1 and multiply the moles of water by -242 kJ/mol.

   _____

   (d) The heat of combustion, ΔH_c of candle wax equals the difference between the products and reactants. Use the following equation to calculate the heat of combustion of your candle.

   $\Delta H_c = (H \text{ products}) - (H \text{ reactants})$.

   _____

▣▶ Chemistry

Heat of Combustion: Candle Wax, continued

Conclusions

1. Is the heat of combustion a positive or negative value?
Explain your answers in terms of endothermic and
exothermic reactions.

_____

_____

_____

2. To calculate the kilojoules, kJ, of heat released in your reaction,
multiply the moles of candle wax burned by the heat of
combustion. _____

_____

3. Look up the word "wick" in a dictionary. How can wick be
used as a noun? How can wick be used a verb?

_____

_____

Explore Further

Design an experiment to show that the candle wax does not burn
with complete combustion or an experiment to show that water is a
product of the combustion of a candle.

Simulating an Entropy Change
Use with Discovery Investigation 13, pages 532–533

Many chemical and physical changes result in more disorder
among particles of matter. In chemistry, the degree of disorder in a
system is called entropy. How can you model changes in entropy?
You will find out in this investigation.

Materials   8 black checkers
              8 red checkers
              tray

Procedure

1. Place two rows of four black checkers in one corner of the tray.
Place two rows of four red checkers next to the black checkers,
as shown.

2. Find a way to cause a small increase in entropy among the
checkers. Do not touch the checkers. Keep them flat on the
tray.

3. Restore the checkers to the initial arrangement of four rows.

4. Find a way to cause a large entropy increase among the
checkers. Again, do not touch the checkers and keep them flat
on the tray.

Cleanup/Disposal

Return all materials. Clean your work area.

Analysis

1. How could you tell that entropy increased in step 2?

_____

2. After step 2, how could you tell that the entropy of the
checkers could increase further?

_____

3. How could you tell that the entropy in step 4 was greater than
the entropy in step 2?

_____

Simulating an Entropy Change, continued

Conclusions

1. Describe the entropy changes modeled in this investigation.

_____

_____

2. After step 4, do you think you could succeed in getting the checkers to return to their initial arrangement without touching them? Explain.

_____

_____

3. How could you get the checkers to return to their initial arrangement?

_____

Explore Further

Use the tray and checkers to model the particle structure of a solid, a liquid, and a gas. Describe the entropy differences among the three states of matter.

_____

_____

_____

Express Lab 14

Use with Express Lab 14, page 548

Materials   safety goggles
lab coat or apron
solid air freshener, in small pieces
small glass bowl with flat bottom
150-mL beaker
plastic cup
ice
hot tap water

Procedure

1. Put on safety goggles and a lab coat or apron.

2. Place a few pieces of air freshener in the beaker, and fill the plastic cup with ice.

3. Place the cup with the ice inside the beaker. The cup should fit snugly inside the beaker but it should not touch the air freshener pieces.

4. Add hot water to the bowl to a depth of about 2.5 cm. Place the beaker assembly in the bowl.

Analysis

1. Describe your observations.

    _____

    _____

2. How can you explain your observations?

    _____

    _____

Crystalline vs. Amorphous Solids

Molecular and ionic crystals are brittle and fracture along orderly
crystal planes. Metallic crystals are soft and do not fracture
when struck. The atoms in a metal slide past each other like
ball bearings immersed in oil. Amorphous solids lack a well-
defined arrangement of particles. They tend to shatter into many
asymmetrical pieces. How do jewelers use knowledge of crystalline
structure when cutting gemstones?

Materials   safety goggles
             lab coat or apron
             magnifying glass
             hammer
             4 small plastic baggies
             one large piece of rock salt
             one lead fishing weight
             one small ice cube
             one small piece of glass tubing

Procedure

1. Put on safety goggles and a lab coat or apron.

2. Collect samples of rock salt, ice, a lead fishing weight, and glass
   tubing. Observe and record the physical characteristics and
   make a drawing of each substance before you tap it.

Crystalline vs. Amorphous Solids, continued

Solid Substance	Description	Before Tapping	After Tapping
rock salt	physical characteristics		
	drawing		
ice cube	physical characteristics		
	drawing		
lead weight	physical characteristics		
	drawing		
glass tubing	physical characteristics		
	drawing		

3. Place the rock salt into a plastic baggie. Tap it gently with the hammer. Observe and record the physical characteristics and make a drawing.

4. Place the ice cube into a plastic baggie. Tap it gently with the hammer. Observe and record the physical characteristics and make a drawing.

5. Place the lead fishing weight into a plastic baggie. Tap it gently with the hammer. Observe and record the physical characteristics and make a drawing.

Crystalline vs. Amorphous Solids, continued

6. Place the glass tubing into a plastic baggie. Tap it gently with the hammer. Observe and record the physical characteristics and make a drawing. **Safety Alert: Handle sharp objects with care.**

Cleanup/Disposal

Return all materials. Clean your work area, and wash your hands.

Analysis

1. What were the similarities between each solid before you tapped them?

_____

_____

2. What were the differences between each solid before you tapped them?

_____

_____

3. What were the similarities between each solid after you tapped them?

_____

_____

4. What were the differences between each solid after you tapped them?

_____

_____

_____

Crystalline vs. Amorphous Solids, continued

Conclusions

Directions Match the items in column A with those in column B.
Write the letter of each correct answer on the line.

Column A	Column B
_____ **1.** ice cube	**A** molecular crystal
_____ **2.** rock salt	**B** amorphous solid
_____ **3.** lead weight	**C** ionic crystal
_____ **4.** glass tubing	**D** metallic solid

Explore Further

Research the different types of crystal structures that occur in
nature. A good place to find this kind of information is in a book
about rocks and minerals. Prepare three-dimensional models of
each crystal type and list examples of the compounds that display
each crystal type.

_____

_____

_____

_____

Graphing a Heating Curve for Water

During phase changes, heat energy is absorbed into the particles. When heated, the particles in a solid begin to absorb energy. They start to move faster, slide past each other, and become a liquid. The same is true when a liquid moves to the gaseous phase. Do you think the temperature of water increases as it melts or boils?

Materials   safety goggles
lab coat or apron
stopwatch or timer
hot plate
small beaker
ice
thermometer
ring stand
buret or test tube clamp
graph paper

Procedure

1. Put on safety goggles and a lab coat or apron.

2. Use the data chart on the next page to record time and temperature. The time column starts with 0. The temperature column is blank. You will record temperatures in the temperature column during the investigation.

Graphing a Heating Curve for Water, continued

Time (min)	Temperature (°C)
0	
0.5	
1.0	
1.5	
2.0	
2.5	
3.0	
3.5	
4.0	
4.5	
5.0	
5.5	
6.0	
6.5	
7.0	
7.5	
8.0	
8.5	
9.0	
9.5	
10.0	
10.5	
11.0	
11.5	
12.0	
12.5	
13.0	
13.5	
14.0	
14.5	
15.0	

Graphing a Heating Curve for Water, continued

3. Fill a small beaker with ice. Insert the thermometer. Wait 2 minutes. Observe and record the starting temperature (0 time) in the data table. **Safety Alert: Handle glass with care. Report any broken or chipped glass to your teacher immediately. Wipe up all spills immediately.**

4. Place the beaker of ice on the hot plate. Position the ring stand and clamp so that the thermometer can be clamped upright in the beaker. The bulb of the thermometer should not touch the bottom of the beaker.

5. Turn the hot plate on high and begin timing. After 0.5 minutes, record the thermometer reading without removing the thermometer from the beaker. **Safety Alert: Use care around hot objects. Report any burns immediately.**

6. Continue recording the temperature every 0.5 minutes for 15 minutes.

Cleanup/Disposal

Wash the glassware, and return all materials. Clean your work area, and wash your hands.

Analysis

Prepare a graph from your data with the following information included:

1. Label the *x*-axis with time as the independent variable and the *y*-axis temperature as the dependent variable.

2. Plot your points using laboratory data. Use a ruler to make straight lines connecting the data points.

3. Label the following five areas on your graph: solid (S), liquid (L), gas (G), freezing/melting point (FP/MP), and condensation/boiling point (CP/BP).

4. Trace, with colored pencils, the following parts of the line on your graph: slowest molecular motion (in red), fastest molecular motion (in green).

Graphing a Heating Curve for Water, continued

Conclusions

Your graph should look like stair steps instead of a straight line.

Explain the presence of the flat areas on your line during the phase changes from solid to liquid and liquid to gas.

_____

_____

Explore Further

Research what is occurring when you have a "fever." What part does water play in regulating your body temperature? What happens to the chemical bonds of enzymes when exposed to too much heat?

_____

_____

_____

The Heat of Fusion of Ice

Use with Investigation 14, pages 563–564

Materials   safety goggles
lab coat or apron
balance
8-oz foam cup
100-mL beaker
warm tap water
thermometer
2 or 3 ice cubes
stirring rod

When ice is added to warm water, the ice melts and the water cools. The mixture eventually reaches a final temperature. The heat released by the warm water equals the heat gained by the ice as it melts. Can you determine the heat of fusion of ice? Find out in this investigation.

Procedure

1. Make a data table like the one shown here.

Variable	Initial Value	Final Value
mass of empty cup (g)		
mass of cup and water (g)		
mass of water (g)		
temperature of water (°C)		

2. Put on safety goggles and a lab coat or apron.

3. Measure and record the mass of the empty cup.

4. Add 100 mL of warm water to the cup.

5. Measure the initial mass of the cup and warm water. Find the mass of the water. Measure the initial water temperature. Record all of these values.

6. Add the ice cubes to the warm water. Do not let any water splash out of the cup.

7. Stir the water until all of the ice melts.

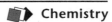

The Heat of Fusion of Ice, continued

8. Measure the final temperature of the water. Measure the final

mass of the cup and water. Find the mass of the water. Record all of these values.

Cleanup/Disposal

Return all equipment. Clean your work area and wash your hands.

Analysis

1. Calculate how much heat the initial mass of water released as it cooled to the final temperature.

_____

2. How many grams of ice melted? Explain your answer.

_____

3. Calculate the amount of heat gained by the melted ice as it warmed from 0°C to the final temperature.

_____

4. Subtract the amount of heat in question 3 from the amount in question 1. The result is the heat needed to melt the ice. Divide this amount by the number of grams of ice. The result is the heat of fusion of ice.

_____

_____

Conclusions

1. How does your value of the heat of fusion of ice compare with the accepted value of 334 J/g?

_____

2. What might be some sources of error in the investigation?

_____

_____

The Heat of Fusion of Ice, continued

Explore Further

Repeat the investigation with a larger cup and twice the amounts of warm water and ice. Is your heat of fusion value closer to the accepted value? Explain your answer.

_____

_____

_____

Melting Dry Ice

Use with Discovery Investigation, pages 571–572

Materials   safety goggles
lab coat or apron
transparent plastic cup
room-temperature water
scissors
plastic pipet
metric ruler
thermal gloves
small scoopula
2–3 g of dry ice (powdered or in small pieces)
pliers

Solid carbon dioxide is called dry ice. It sublimes at room temperature and pressure, as the phase diagram below shows. However, CO_2 exists as a liquid at a pressure greater than its triple-point pressure. Can you observe liquid CO_2? You will explore this question in this investigation.

Procedure

1. Read the entire procedure. Study the phase diagram on the next page.

2. Make a table to record your observations. Write a hypothesis about what changes will occur during the investigation.

3. Put on safety goggles and a lab coat or apron.

4. Half-fill the cup with water.

5. Carefully cut the tip off the pipet so the stem is about 7 cm long.

6. Put on thermal gloves. Use the scoopula to place enough dry ice into the pipet to fill the bulb halfway. **Safety Alert: Do not touch dry ice. Wear thermal gloves when working with dry ice.**

7. Clamp the pliers over the open end of the pipet so that no gas escapes. Hold the pipet by the pliers and lower the bulb into the water. Observe and record what happens to the dry ice.

Melting Dry Ice, continued

8. When you see liquid form in the bulb of the pipet, release the pressure on the pliers, while still holding the pipet in the water. Record your observations.

9. Again clamp the pliers on the end of the pipet. Watch for liquid to form, then release the pressure. Repeat this step, observing all changes that occur.

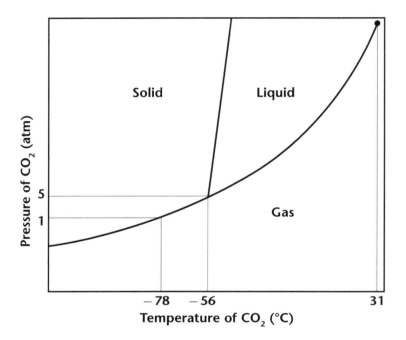

Cleanup/Disposal

Return or dispose of the materials. Clean your work area, and wash your hands.

Analysis

1. What was the purpose of the pliers?

_____

_____

2. Why was the bulb of the pipet placed in water?

_____

_____

Melting Dry Ice, continued

3. How did the CO_2 change throughout the investigation?

_____

_____

Conclusions

1. Was the pressure inside the pipet greater than the triple-point pressure of CO_2? Explain your answer.

_____

2. Describe what happens to dry ice as it warms at various pressures.

_____

_____

Explore Further

What do you predict will happen if you fill the pipet bulb three-quarters full with dry ice? Test your prediction.

_____

_____

Express Lab 15

Use with Express Lab 15, page 582

Materials   safety goggles
lab coat or apron
3 100-mL beakers
150-mL of distilled water
25 g of sugar ($C_{12}H_{22}O_{11}$)
25 g of calcium carbonate ($CaCO_3$)
25 g of table salt ($NaCl$)
stirring rod

Procedure

1. Put on safety goggles and a lab coat or apron.

2. Pour 50 mL of distilled water into each beaker. **Safety Alert: Be careful when working with glassware.**

3. Pour the sugar into one beaker. Stir until all of the solute is dissolved.

4. Record your observations.

5. Repeat steps 3 and 4 with the other two solutes.

Analysis

1. Which solute was most soluble in water? Explain your answer.

_____

_____

2. Which solute was least soluble in water? Explain your answer.

_____

_____

Solubility and Temperature

Use with Investigation 15, pages 591–592

Solubility usually varies with solvent temperature. How does
water temperature affect the solubility of potassium nitrate? In
this investigation, you will measure the temperatures at which
quantities of KNO_3 dissolve. You will then construct a solubility
curve from your data.

Materials   safety goggles
            lab coat or apron
            metal pan
            tap water
            hot plate
            ring stand
            beaker clamp
            thermometer clamp
            100-mL beaker
            65 g of potassium nitrate (KNO_3)
            balance
            distilled water
            stirring rod
            thermometer
            beaker tongs
            graph paper

Procedure

1. Put on safety goggles and a lab coat or apron.

2. Pour tap water into the pan. Set the pan on the hot plate.

3. Set up the ring stand and clamps beside the hot plate.

4. Measure out one 25-g and four 10-g samples of KNO_3 on the
   balance. Set these samples aside. **Safety Alert: Keep the KNO_3
   away from the hot plate even though the hot plate is turned
   off at this point.**

5. Pour 50 mL of distilled water into the beaker. Add the 25 g of
   KNO_3. Stir the solution with the stirring rod until no more
   solute dissolves. Some solute will not dissolve.

Solubility and Temperature, continued

6. Place the beaker in its clamp and lower it halfway into the tap water. Place the thermometer in its clamp and lower the bulb into the solution. Turn on the hot plate to medium. **Safety Alert: Do not touch heated objects with your hands.**

7. Stir the solution until the solute has completely dissolved. Record the solution temperature.

8. Add a 10-g KNO_3 sample to the solution. Stir the solution until the solute has completely dissolved. Record the temperature.

9. Repeat step 8 for the remaining 10-g samples.

10. Turn off the hot plate and let the water in the pan cool.

11. Use your data to make a solubility curve on graph paper. Plot temperature on the *x*-axis. Plot KNO_3 mass per 50 mL of water on the *y*-axis.

Cleanup/Disposal

Use the beaker tongs to pour the solution into a proper waste container. Pour the water down the sink. Return equipment and clean your work area. Wash your hands.

Analysis

1. What does the shape of the solubility curve show? _____

2. Does the solubility curve show a large or small temperature dependence? _____

Conclusions

1. How much KNO_3 will dissolve in 50 mL of water at 55°C? _____

2. Is KNO_3 slightly soluble, soluble, or highly soluble in water? Justify your answer. _____

Explore Further

Repeat the investigation using sodium chloride, NaCl, as the solute.

Mixing Up Solutions

At a doctor's office, patients are often asked to supply a sample of urine or blood. Several tests are done to determine dissolved solutes in these solutions. Levels of such things as sodium, iron, albumin, and glucose help determine health. How is the concentration of a solute in a solution calculated? In this investigation, you will find out.

Materials   safety goggles
                lab coat or apron
                solid NaCl
                100-mL volumetric flask
                electronic balance (to 350 g or higher)
                small beaker
                distilled water

Procedure

1. Put on safety goggles and a lab coat or apron.

2. Place the volumetric flask on the balance. Press the tare button. The display should read 0.00. The balance will ignore the mass of the volumetric flask. Do not remove the flask. Add 10.0 g of NaCl to the flask. Record this measurement in the chart below. **Digital balances are extremely accurate and sensitive measuring devices. Do not press on the pan. Avoid spilling on it.**

Mass of NaCl Added to Flask (g)	Moles of NaCl Added to Flask (mol)	Mass of Water Added to Flask (kg)	Moles of Water Added to Flask (mol)	Total Volume of Solution (mL)	Total Mass of Solution (g)
				100.0 mL	

Mixing Up Solutions, continued

3. Convert the grams to moles. Record this in the chart.

4. Tare the balance with the volumetric flask containing NaCl. Add distilled water to the flask until it's half full. Swirl to dissolve the solute and return the flask to the balance. Continue to add water until the solution reaches the 100-mL mark on the flask's neck. Record the mass of water (in kilograms) added to the flask. Record the total mass of the solution.

5. Swirl until all solute is dissolved.

Cleanup/Disposal

Wash the glassware, and return all materials. Clean your work area, and wash your hands.

Analysis

1. Calculate the mass percent of your solution. Use the formula,

$$\text{mass percent} = \frac{\text{g solute}}{\text{g solution}}$$

_____

2. Calculate the mole fraction of your solution. Use the formula,

$$\text{mole fraction} = \frac{\text{moles of solute}}{\text{total moles in solution}}$$

_____

3. Calculate the molality (m) of your solution. Use the formula,

$$m = \frac{\text{moles of solute}}{\text{kg of solvent}}$$

_____

4. Calculate the molarity (M) of your solution. Use the formula,

$$M = \frac{\text{moles of solute}}{\text{liters of solvent}}$$

_____

Mixing Up Solutions, continued

Conclusions

1. Think back on the various labs you have done in chemistry. Which unit of concentration has appeared frequently on the bottles of solutions? _____

2. Another concentration expression is density. Density tells how many grams of solution are in 1 mL of solution. Calculate the density of your solution using mass/volume.

_____

Explore Further

Certain health agencies are responsible for regulating clean water and air standards. Particles and contaminants are often listed in parts per million, or ppm. Contact your local water supplier and ask for a copy of their water quality report. Analyze it and report on your findings.

Colligative Properties of Water: Boiling-Point Elevation

Adding a solute to a pure liquid changes the properties of the liquid. One example is mixing antifreeze with your car's coolant water. This prevents the water from boiling over in summer and freezing up in winter. Seawater in arctic areas does not freeze, yet icebergs are big chunks of ice floating in seawater. Some cooks add salt to the water before it boils. What do all of these situations have in common?

Materials safety goggles
      lab coat or apron
      250-mL beaker
      digital balance
      table salt
      distilled water
      graduated cylinder
      stirring rod
      thermometer

Procedure

1. Put on safety goggles and a lab coat or apron.

2. Copy the table on the next page on your paper. Record your observations in the table.

3. Place the beaker on the balance and tare. Add 5.0 g of salt. Remove the beaker from the balance. **Safety Alert: Handle glass with care. Report any broken or chipped glass to your teacher immediately. Wipe up all spills immediately. Digital balances are extremely accurate and sensitive measuring devices. Do not press on the pan.**

4. Add 95.0 mL of distilled water and stir. This solution has a 5.0% NaCl concentration.

5. Place the beaker on the hot plate and begin heating. Once it comes to a full, rolling boil, place your thermometer into the solution. Wait 2 minutes and then record the temperature at boiling in the data table. **Safety Alert: Use care around hot objects. Report any burns immediately.**

Colligative Properties of Water:
Boiling-Point Elevation, continued

Solution Concentration	Temperature at Boiling	Change in Boiling Point
5.0% NaCl		
10% NaCl		
25% NaCl		

6. Dispose of the solution down the drain. Rinse the beaker thoroughly.

7. Repeat steps 4 and 5 with 10.0 g of salt and 90.0 mL of distilled water. This solution has a 10% NaCl concentration.

8. Repeat steps 4 and 5 with 25.0 g of salt and 75.0 mL of distilled water. This solution has a 25% NaCl concentration.

Cleanup/Disposal

Wash the glassware, and return all materials. Clean your work area, and wash your hands.

Analysis

1. What effect did adding salt have on the boiling point of water?

_____

2. What is the relationship between the amount of solute (concentration) and the effect on boiling point?

_____

_____

3. Calculate the K_b for the water using one set of data from your chart. Use the formulas and instructions given in your text (Chapter 15, Lesson 6). Determine your percent error if the accurate value is 0.51°C/m for water. The formula for percent error is:

$$\text{percent error} = \frac{\text{difference between your } Kb \text{ value and the accepted } Kb \text{ value}}{\text{accepted } Kb \text{ value}} \times 100\,\%$$

Colligative Properties of Water:
Boiling-Point Elevation, continued

Conclusions

1. Why do cooks add salt to water?

_____

_____

2. What other practical uses are there for increasing the boiling
point of a substance?

_____

Explore Further

Research and report your finding on the effect altitude has on
cooking. Go to the grocery store and look on boxes of cake mix for
baking adjustments.

Freezing-Point Depression

Use with Discovery Investigation 15, pages 613–614

A solution does not freeze at the same temperature as the pure
solvent. This is because solute and solvent particles interact,
reducing the ability of the solvent particles to freeze. How much
does solute concentration affect the freezing point of a solution? In
this investigation, you will measure the freezing point of solutions
of different concentrations.

Materials
safety goggles
lab coat or apron
600-mL beaker
small ice cubes or crushed ice
rock salt
ring stand
test-tube clamp

4 large test tubes
25 g of calcium chloride ($CaCl_2$)
balance
200 mL of distilled water
stirring rod
thermometer
graph paper

Procedure

1. Write a hypothesis predicting how the freezing point will vary
   for four different aqueous solutions of $CaCl_2$.

2. Write a procedure to test your hypothesis. In your procedure,
   describe how you plan to vary the $CaCl_2$ concentration. Also
   describe how you plan to use ice and rock salt to freeze the test
   solutions. Include any safety alerts.

3. Have your hypothesis and procedure approved by your
   teacher.

4. Perform your procedure and record your data. Be sure to wear
   safety goggles and a lab coat or apron.

5. Graph your data. Plot concentration on the *x*-axis and
   temperature on the *y*-axis.

Freezing-Point Depression, continued

Cleanup/Disposal

Pour the solutions into the proper waste container. Pour the ice and saltwater mixture down the sink. Wash and dry the glassware and return all equipment. Wash your hands.

Analysis

1. What information does your graph show? _____

2. How does freezing point vary with concentration? Is your plot
a straight line or a curve? _____

_____

3. How were you able to make the ice bath colder than the
freezing point of ice? _____

Conclusions

1. Suppose a 50-mL aqueous solution contains 12.5 g of $CaCl_2$.
At what temperature do you predict this solution will freeze?
Use your graph to find your answer. _____

2. Suppose your graph was flatter (more horizontal). What
would this show? _____

3. Suppose you measured the boiling points of the four solutions.
Which solution would you expect to have the highest boiling
point? _____

Explore Further

Using ice and different amounts of rock salt, measure freezing-point depressions for the ice bath. Try to find the lowest temperature to which the freezing point can be reduced.

Express Lab 16

Use with Express Lab 16, page 624

Materials   safety goggles
lab coat or apron
3 effervescent antacid tablets
3 plastic cups
cold, hot, and room-temperature water
watch or clock with a second hand

Procedure

1. Put on safety goggles and a lab coat or apron.

2. Fill one plastic cup with hot water, one with room-temperature water, and one with cold water.

3. Drop an antacid tablet in the cup of hot water. Record the time.

4. Wait until the tablet has disappeared, then record the time again.

5. Repeat steps 3 and 4 with the other cups.

Analysis

1. How did the water temperature affect the amount of time required for each tablet to disappear?

_____

_____

2. What result would you expect if you placed a tablet in ice water? In boiling water?

_____

_____

Name Date Period

Lab Manual, Page 1

Factors Influencing Reaction Rate

Several different factors can change the rate at which a chemical reaction will occur. These include the type of reactants, the surface area of reactants, the concentration of the reactants, the temperature of the system, and the presence of any catalysts. Can you think of an example of each in your everyday life?

Materials safety goggles
lab coat or apron
Bunsen burner
small piece of copper
small piece of zinc
4 small pieces of magnesium
steel wool
steel paper clip
acetic acid
6 test tubes
test tube rack
10-mL graduated cylinder

Procedure

1. Put on safety goggles and a lab coat or apron.

2. Add 10 mL of acetic acid to three test tubes. **Safety Alert: Handle glass with care. Report any broken or chipped glass to your teacher immediately. Wipe up all spills immediately. Acetic acid is caustic and has a pungent "vinegar" smell. Avoid contact.**

3. To tube #1, add one piece of copper. To tube #2, add one piece of zinc. To tube #3, add one piece of magnesium. Record your observations in the table on page 2. Compare the reaction rates for each metal.

Factors Influencing Reaction Rate, continued

Test Tube	Reaction	Observations	Comparison
#1	acetic acid + Mg		
#2	acetic acid + Cu		
#3	acetic acid + Zn		
#4	10 mL acetic acid + Mg		
#5	5 mL acetic acid + 5 mL H_2O + Mg		
#6	2.5 mL acetic acid + 7.5 mL H_2O + Mg		
	Steel paper clip in Bunsen burner		
	Steel wool ball in Bunsen burner		

4. In test tube #4 place 10 mL acetic acid. In test tube #5 place 5 mL acetic acid and 5 mL distilled water. In test tube #6 place 2.5 mL acetic acid and 7.5 mL distilled water.

5. Next, add one piece of magnesium to test tubes #4–#6. Record your observations. Compare the reaction rates for the three solutions.

6. Using the tongs, hold the steel paper clip in the hottest part of the burner flame for 30 seconds. **Safety Alert: Use care around hot objects. Report any burns immediately.** Repeat with a piece of steel wool that you've fluffed up. Record your observations. Compare the reaction rate for the two steel objects.

Cleanup/Disposal

Wash the glassware, and return all materials. Clean your work area, and wash your hands.

Analysis

1. Which reaction involved the surface area of the metal?

_____

Factors Influencing Reaction Rate, continued

2. Which reaction involved changing the type of reactants?

_____

3. Which reaction involved changing the concentration of the
reactant? _____

4. You tested three different rate-influencing factors. Name two
other factors that influence reaction rate.

_____

Conclusions

1. Why does increasing the surface area usually increase the
reaction rate?

_____

2. Why did one kind of metal react faster with acetic acid than
the others? (Hint: Look at an Activity Series of Metals. Think
about the atomic structure and valence electrons of each
metal.)

_____

3. Why does increasing the concentration of a solution usually
increase the reaction rate?

_____

Explore Further

Write the balanced chemical equation for the reaction between
acetic acid ($HC_2H_3O_2$) and magnesium metal. A gas was generated.
Which gas was it? With your teacher's permission, repeat the
investigation above, collect the gas, and test it with a wood splint.

_____

_____

How a Catalyst Affects a Chemical Reaction

Use with Investigation 16, pages 633–634

Catalysts change the behavior of chemical reactions. One catalyst
is manganese dioxide. It is insoluble in water. Another catalyst
is an enzyme called catalase or peroxidase. This enzyme is in
animal tissues and certain vegetables. How do these catalysts
affect the decomposition of hydrogen peroxide? Find out in this
investigation.

Materials   safety goggles   matches
                       lab coat or apron   3 medium test tubes
                       50 mL of 3% hydrogen peroxide (H_2O_2) solution   test-tube rack
                            in a 100-mL beaker   spatula
                       0.1 g of manganese dioxide (MnO_2)   grease pencil
                       radish or potato, finely chopped   metric ruler
                       wood splints

Procedure

1. Put on safety goggles and a lab coat or apron.

2. Using the grease pencil, place a line about 3 cm from the
   bottom of each test tube. Label the test tubes 1, 2, and 3.
   Place them in the rack.

3. Use the spatula to place enough of the chopped vegetable
   into test tube 1 to reach the line.

4. Add the manganese dioxide to test tube 2. Leave test
   tube 3 empty.

5. Slowly pour hydrogen peroxide solution into tube 1 until it
   reaches the line. **Safety Alert: Hydrogen peroxide can bleach
   clothing. Handle it carefully.**

6. Observe the contents in the test tube and record your
   observations.

7. Wait until any observed reaction slows down. Then light the
   end of a splint with a match. Blow out the flame, leaving the
   end of the splint glowing. **Safety Alert: Be careful with the
   match and flame.**

8. Quickly place the glowing splint into the mouth of test
   tube 1. Observe and record the result. If a flame is produced,
   completely extinguish the splint before proceeding.

How a Catalyst Affects a Chemical Reaction, continued

9. Repeat steps 5 through 8 with test tube 2 and then with test tube 3.

Cleanup/Disposal

Dispose of the cooled matches and splints. Dispose of the test tube contents as your teacher directs. Clean and return the other materials. Wash your hands.

Analysis

1. Describe what happened when hydrogen peroxide was added to each test tube.

_____

_____

2. What happened when the glowing splint was put into each tube?

_____

_____

Conclusions

1. What was the purpose of test tube 3, which contained only hydrogen peroxide?

_____

2. What was given off by the catalyzed reactions? How do you know?

_____

_____

3. Write the balanced equation for the decomposition of hydrogen peroxide.

_____

Explore Further

Repeat the experiment with other fresh plant materials. Which ones produce results similar to the plant material you used in the above investigation, and which ones do not?

_____

_____

_____

What's Equal About Equilibrium?

When you get off a whirling amusement-park ride, you might feel a little dizzy. You would probably pause a few minutes to "get your equilibrium" back. You might also call this balance, but does this mean equal? Does chemical equilibrium mean there are equal amounts of reactants and products?

Materials safety goggles
                  lab coat or apron
                  100-mL beaker
                  100-mL graduated cylinder

2 glass tubes of equal diameter, longer than the graduated cylinder, and open at both ends

Procedure

1. Put on safety goggles and a lab coat or apron.

2. Measure 20 mL of water in the graduated cylinder and pour it into the beaker. **Safety Alert: Handle glass with care. Report any broken or chipped glass to your teacher immediately. Wipe up all spills immediately.**

3. Fill the graduated cylinder to the 20-mL mark and place near the beaker.

4. Place a glass tube in the graduated cylinder and in the beaker. Allow them to collect water.

5. Using your fingers, cover the ends of both glass tubes with separate hands. At the same time, and without losing any water, swap the glass tubes. The glass tube originally in the graduated cylinder is now in the beaker, and vice versa. Release the glass tubes.

6. Observe the volume of water in the graduated cylinder and in the beaker. Record the volume of each under swap number 1.

swap number	0	1	2	3	4	5	6	7	8	9	10	11	12	13	14	15	16	17	18	19	20
graduated cylinder volume (mL)	20																				
beaker volume (mL)	20																				

What's Equal About Equilibrium?, continued

7. Repeat the transfer process 19 more times. Record the
changing water levels in the graduated cylinder and beaker
each time you swap the glass tubes.

Cleanup/Disposal

Wash the glassware, and return all materials. Clean your work area,
and wash your hands.

Analysis

1. Compare the heights of water in the two glass tubes during
the first swap. Which glass tube had more water? Explain your
answer. _____

_____

2. How did the heights of water in the two tubes compare during
the final swap? _____

3. In the end, the water levels in the graduated cylinder and the
beaker were different. Describe this difference.

_____

_____

Conclusions

Explain your observations during the transfer process in terms of
equilibrium. Include concepts of rate and balance.

_____

_____

Explore Further

The investigation demonstrated a type of physical equilibrium.
Invent a new demonstration using a ball, wooden plank, and
large straw to blow through. You may also choose other materials.
Demonstrate your example to the class or draw diagrams to explain
your procedure.

Le Chatelier's Principle

Use with Discovery Investigation 16, pages 655–656

According to Le Chatelier's principle, when a stress is applied to a reaction at equilibrium, the equilibrium changes to relieve the stress. How can you demonstrate Le Chatelier's principle? In this investigation, you will apply stress to an equilibrium system and observe what happens.

Materials   safety goggles   concentrated hydrochloric acid (HCl)
              lab coat or apron   in a dropper bottle
              gloves   10 mL of distilled water
              2 250-mL beakers   eyedropper
              2 mL of 0.1 M cobalt(II) chloride ($CoCl_2$)   hot plate
                solution in a medium test tube   tap water
              test-tube rack   cup of ice

Procedure

1. Put on safety goggles, a lab coat or apron, and gloves.

2. Record the color of the $CoCl_2$ solution.

3. Add concentrated HCl to the $CoCl_2$ solution, one drop at a time, until a color change occurs. Then add 5 more drops of HCl. Record your observations. **Safety Alert: Concentrated HCl can burn skin and clothing. Handle it carefully. Report any spills immediately. Do not inhale the HCl vapor.**

4. Add distilled water to the same solution, drop by drop, until the color changes again. Record your observations.

5. Slowly add drops of concentrated HCl just until the solution becomes purple. This color should be about halfway between the two colors you observed already.

6. Remove your gloves and goggles. Write a procedure to test the effect of temperature on this solution. Use the materials provided. Include safety alerts.

7. Have your procedure approved by your teacher. Then put on gloves and goggles. Carry out your procedure and record your results.

Le Chatelier's Principle, continued

Cleanup/Disposal

Turn off the hot plate and allow it to cool. Dispose of the solution in a proper waste container. Then clean the glassware and return all materials. Wash your hands.

Analysis

1. What was the color of the starting solution (step 2)? _____

2. What was the solution color after HCl was added (step 3)? _____

3. What was the solution color after water was added (step 4)? _____

4. What was the solution color at equilibrium (step 5)? _____

5. How did temperature affect the color of the solution? _____

Conclusions

The equation for the equilibrium reaction is as follows:
$$CoCl_4^{2-}(aq) + 6H_2O(l) \rightleftarrows Co(H_2O)_6^{2+}(aq) + 4Cl^{1-}(aq) + heat$$

1. There are two cobalt-containing ions in this reaction. How does each one affect the color of the solution? Explain your answer.

_____

_____

2. Why is the solution color affected by temperature?

_____

3. Silver nitrate reacts with chloride ions to form insoluble silver chloride (AgCl). How would adding silver nitrate change the equilibrium of the above reaction? Explain your answer.

_____

_____

Explore Further

A simple weather indicator consists of a strip of paper that has been soaked in $CoCl_2$ solution and allowed to dry. The color of the paper changes according to the humidity. Predict the color of the indicator in moist and dry air. Explain your predictions.

_____

_____

_____

▶ **Chemistry**

Express Lab 17
Use with Express Lab 17, page 667

Materials   safety goggles   blue litmus strip
             lab coat or apron   zinc piece
             6 test tubes   aluminum piece
             test-tube rack   marble chip
             30 mL of 3 *M* HCl   raw egg white
             10-mL graduated cylinder   grease pencil
             bromthymol blue

Procedure

1. Put on safety goggles and a lab coat or apron.

2. Pour 5 mL of HCl into each test tube. Place the test tubes in the rack. Number the tubes 1 to 6.

3. Dip the litmus strip into tube 1.

4. Add a drop of bromthymol blue to tube 2.

5. Add a piece of zinc to tube 3.

6. Add a piece of aluminum to tube 4.

7. Marble is a carbonate. Add a marble chip to tube 5.

8. Egg white is protein. Add egg white to tube 6.

Analysis

1. Describe your observations of each tube.

   _____

   _____

2. How can you explain your observations?

   _____

   _____

Titration of Eggshell

A hen sits on her eggs to incubate the developing embryos. If there is not enough $CaCO_3$ in the eggshells, the hen's weight can crush the eggs. Farmers routinely have the quality of the eggshells checked by chemists. Strong eggshells mean the farmer's chickens are healthy. What factors may cause the eggshells to be deficient in calcium carbonate?

Materials   safety goggles   250-mL Erlenmeyer flask
                lab coat or apron   electronic balance
                two 50-mL burets   crushed eggshells (clean and dry)
                two 100-mL beakers   pipet
                3.0 *M* HCl   distilled water
                3.0 *M* NaOH   phenolphthalein

Procedure

1. Make a data table like the one shown on page 2. Record your observations.

2. Put on safety goggles and a lab coat or apron.

3. Rinse and fill one buret with 3.0 *M* HCl. Place a beaker beneath its tip. Label the beaker "HCl." **Safety Alert: Handle glass with care. Report any broken or chipped glass to your teacher immediately. Wipe up all spills immediately.**

4. Rinse and fill a second buret with 3.0 *M* NaOH. Place a beaker beneath its tip. Label the beaker "NaOH."

Mass of Eggshells (g)	HCl added to Eggshells	NaOH added to Eggshell-Acid
	mL	mL
	L	L

Titration of Eggshell, continued

5. Place the Erlenmeyer flask on the digital balance and tare its mass. Place the flask on the balance. Press the tare button. The display should read 0.00. The balance will ignore the mass of the flask. Do not remove the flask. Measure and record the mass of 0.50 g of the ground eggshell in the flask. **Safety Alert: Digital balances are extremely accurate and sensitive measuring devices. Do not press on the pan. Avoid spilling on it.**

6. Using the buret containing HCl, add 17 to 20 mL to the flask containing eggshells. Record the exact amount of acid added to the flask in the data table. Convert the value to liters.

7. Gently swirl the flask until all bubbling has stopped. This may take several minutes.

8. Using a pipet, wash down the sides of the flask with a small amount of distilled water. Add 2 drops of phenolphthalein indicator to the solution in the flask.

9. Using the buret containing NaOH, titrate the eggshell-acid solution. Allow the NaOH to slowly mix with the eggshell-acid solution until a very pale pink color remains.

10. Measure and record the amount of base added to the eggshell-acid in the data table. Convert this amount into liters.

Cleanup/Disposal

Wash the glassware, and return all materials. Clean your work area, and wash your hands.

Analysis

Calculate the amount of calcium carbonate in the eggshell by following these steps:

1. liters of HCl that reacted with $CaCO_3$ = liters of HCl added to eggshell – liters of NaOH

How many liters of HCl reacted with the eggshell's $CaCO_3$?

_____

Titration of Eggshell, continued

2. moles of HCl reacted = liters HCl that reacted with
$CaCO_3 \times 3.0\ M$ HCl
How many moles of HCl reacted with the eggshell's $CaCO_3$?

_____

3. moles $CaCO_3$ = moles of HCl reacted $\times \dfrac{1\text{ mole of } CaCO_3}{2\text{ moles of HCl}}$
How many moles of $CaCO_3$ were in your eggshell?

_____

4. grams $CaCO_3$ = moles of $CaCO_3 \times \dfrac{100.09\text{ g of } CaCO_3}{1\text{ mole of } CaCO_3}$
How many grams of $CaCO_3$ were in your eggshell?

_____

5. percent $CaCO_3$ in the eggshell = grams of $CaCO_3 \times \dfrac{100}{\text{grams of eggshell}}$

What is the percent of $CaCO_3$ in the eggshell? _____

Conclusions

1. Normal, healthy chickens lay eggs that contain about 85%
$CaCO_3$. How does your % $CaCO_3$ compare?

_____

2. Did your eggshell come from a healthy or unhealthy chicken?

_____

_____

3. What events might cause a chicken's eggshell to be low in
$CaCO_3$?

_____

_____

Explore Further

Many years ago, the pesticide DDT was found to harm the eggshells
of eagles. How did the DDT get into the eagles' eggshells? What
harm did this do to the eggshells? Describe what was done to
prevent this from happening to future eagle populations.

_____

_____

_____

Titrating the Acid in Vinegar
Use with Investigation 17, pages 674–675

When apple cider ferments, it sometimes forms acetic acid, $HC_2H_3O_2$. Vinegar is dilute acetic acid. Can you use titration to find the molarity of the acetic acid in vinegar? You will find out in this investigation.

Materials   safety goggles
lab coat or apron
gloves
3 125-mL Erlenmeyer flasks
2 100-mL beakers
2 50-mL burets
buret clamp
ring stand
80 mL of distilled white vinegar
phenolphthalein solution in a dropper bottle
80 mL of standardized NaOH solution
piece of white paper
grease pencil
distilled water
10-mL graduated cylinder

Procedure

1. To record your data, make a data table like the one shown below.

	Vinegar (mL)			NaOH Solution (mL)		
Trial	Initial Buret Reading	Final Buret Reading	Volume Used	Initial Buret Reading	Final Buret Reading	Volume Used
1						
2						
3						

2. Put on safety goggles, a lab coat or apron, and gloves.

Titrating the Acid in Vinegar, continued

3. Label one beaker and one buret *NaOH;* label the other beaker and buret *vinegar.* Use the two beakers to get about 80 mL each of the vinegar and the NaOH solution. Set up the burets as shown on the next page. Fill them according to your teacher's instructions. **Safety Alert: Be careful when working with glassware and the solutions. Avoid skin contact with the solutions.**

4. In your data table, record the initial readings of both burets. Use the vinegar buret to add approximately 10 mL of vinegar to a flask. Record the final reading of this buret. Add about 10 mL of distilled water and two drops of phenolphthalein to the vinegar in the flask.

5. Use the NaOH buret to add the standardized solution to the vinegar solution in a slow, steady stream of drops, while gently swirling the flask. When the pink color in the flask begins to last longer, add the NaOH solution one drop at a time, swirling the flask between drops.

6. When the pink color remains in the solution, stop adding NaOH. You have reached the end point. Record the final reading of the NaOH buret.

7. Repeat the procedure two more times using the other flasks.

Cleanup/Disposal

Clean the glassware and return the equipment. Dispose of the solutions in a proper waste container. Clean your work area and wash your hands.

Titrating the Acid in Vinegar, continued

Analysis

1. From the buret readings, calculate the NaOH volume and vinegar volume used in each trial.

   _____

   _____

2. What is the molarity of the standardized NaOH? For each trial, calculate the molarity of the vinegar.

   _____

   _____

3. What is the average molarity of the vinegar? Why is it useful to have more than one trial and average the results?

   _____

   _____

Conclusions

1. Why is it important for a producer of vinegar to check its molarity?

   _____

2. Why could you add water to the vinegar sample without changing the results?

   _____

Explore Further

Repeat the investigation with wine vinegar or cider vinegar. What problem do you have that you did not have with white vinegar?

   _____

   _____

Chemistry

Water into Milk

Color changes often accompany pH changes in a substance. A quick analysis of a swimming pool or soil sample involves different substances and many color changes. Even a urine test in a doctor's office involves pH and color changes. What other tests involve pH and color changes?

Materials
safety goggles
lab coat or apron
6 clean cups
100-mL graduated cylinder
10-mL graduated cylinder
distilled water
2 pipets
phenolphthalein
0.10 M NaOH

6 M NaOH
9 M H_2SO_4
$NaHCO_3$
saturated barium nitrate solution
glass stirring rod
electronic balance
red and blue litmus paper
permanent marker

Procedure

1. Put on safety goggles and a lab coat or apron.

2. Set up and label six clean cups as follows:

   Cup #1: 100 mL of distilled water mixed with 2 drops of phenolphthalein

   Cup #2: 5 drops of 0.10 M sodium hydroxide

   Cup #3: 15–16 drops of 9 M sulfuric acid

   Cup #4: 0.50 g of sodium bicarbonate mixed with 1–2 mL (22–44 drops) of distilled water

   Cup #5: 4–5 mL of saturated barium nitrate solution

   Cup #6: 2–3 mL of 6 M sodium hydroxide

   Safety Alert: Avoid getting chemicals on your skin or in your mouth. If this happens, report it immediately.

Water into Milk, continued

3. Fill each cup with the correct substances before you begin.

4. Mix the contents of cup #1 with the stirring rod.

5. Record your observations in the data table below. Test cup #1 with both red and blue litmus papers. Record whether the solution is acidic, basic, or neutral in the data table.

6. Rinse and dry the stirring rod.

Cup	Observations	Acidic, Basic, or Neutral
#1		
#1 into #2		
#2 into #3		
#3 into #4		
#4 into #5		
#5 into #6		

7. Pour the contents of cup #1 into cup #2 and repeat steps 4 and 5.

8. Continue by pouring the combined solutions into the next cup and repeating steps 4 and 5.

Cleanup/Disposal

Flush the final solution down the drain and allow the water to run for 2 minutes. Throw the cups in the trash. Return all other materials. Clean your work area, and wash your hands.

Analysis

The reactions for this investigation are below. Write the correct formulas for the products and balance the equations.

1. _____ $NaOH$ + _____ $H_2SO_4 \rightarrow$
   _____ _____ + _____ _____

2. _____ H_2SO_4 + _____ $NaHCO_3 \rightarrow$
   _____ _____ + _____ _____ + _____ H_2O

Water into Milk, continued

3. _____ Na_2SO_4 + _____ $Ba(NO_3)_2 \rightarrow$
_____ _____ + _____ _____

4. Name the gas that caused the bubbling when cup #3 was poured into cup #4. (Hint: Look at reaction 2 above.)

_____

5. What is the name of the white precipitate that formed when you added cup #4 to #5? (Hint: Look at problem 3 above, and a solubility table.)

_____

Conclusions

1. What color was usually observed when acids were present in the cups?

_____

2. What color was usually observed when bases were present in the cups?

_____

3. What color was usually observed when there was a neutral solution present in the cups?

_____

4. Why would a pH meter be better for giving more accurate data? Why would we need more accurate data about the solutions in the cups?

_____

_____

Explore Further

Go to a pool or spa supply store. Locate the water testing kits. Discuss with an employee how the test kits work. Report back to the class on your findings.

Strong and Weak Acids
Use with Discovery Investigation, pages 686–687

Strong acids completely ionize in water. Weak acids ionize
only slightly. How well do acidic solutions conduct an electric
current? In this investigation, you will relate the strengths and
concentrations of acids to their electrical conductivity.

Materials   safety goggles
lab coat or apron
gloves
100 mL of 2.0 M acetic acid ($HC_2H_3O_2$)
100 mL of 2.0 M hydrochloric acid (HCl)
6 100-mL beakers
50-mL graduated cylinder
distilled water
wash bottle
conductivity tester
grease pencil

Procedure

1. You will determine how well six acid solutions conduct a
   current by whether a lightbulb in a circuit lights up brightly,
   dimly, or not at all. Read the entire procedure. Then make a
   table you can use to record your data.

2. The equation, $M_1V_1 = M_2V_2$, can be used to make dilutions.
   Write a procedure to show how you can make 100 mL each
   of 1.0 M HCl and 1.0 M $HC_2H_3O_2$ from the 2.0 M solutions.
   Then write a procedure for making 100 mL each of 0.10 M
   HCl and 0.10 M $HC_2H_3O_2$ from the 1.0 M solutions. Include
   safety alerts in your procedure.

3. Have your teacher approve your procedure.

4. Put on safety goggles, a lab coat or apron, and gloves. **Safety
   Alert: Acids can damage skin and clothing.**

5. Prepare the four new solutions according to your procedure.
   Use labeled beakers to store the six solutions.

Strong and Weak Acids, continued

6. Use the conductivity tester to test each solution. For each test, record the brightness of the bulb in your data table. Wash the wires of the tester with distilled water between tests.

Cleanup/Disposal

Wash the glassware and return all equipment. Dispose of the solutions according to your teacher's instructions. Clean your work area and wash your hands.

Analysis

1. For which solutions did the bulb burn brightly?

_____

_____

2. As the concentration of the HCl and $HC_2H_3O_2$ decreased, what happened to the conductivity?

_____

Conclusions

1. Explain why the concentration of an acid affects its conductivity.

_____

2. Based on your data, is hydrochloric acid strong or weak? Is acetic acid strong or weak?

_____

Explore Further

List common acidic solutions you have at home. Predict whether these acids are strong or weak. If your teacher approves, use the conductivity tester to test these solutions.

_____

_____

Express Lab 18
Use with Express Lab 18, page 704

Procedure

1. In this lab, you will practice using the rules for determining oxidation numbers. On a sheet of paper, copy the table below.

2. Fill in the missing oxidation numbers.

Substance	Oxidation Numbers
I_2	$I = ?$
H_2O	$O = ?, H = ?$
$NaClO_4$	$O = ?, Na = ?, Cl = ?$
$Ca_3(PO_4)_2$	$Ca = ?, P = ?, O = ?$

Analysis

1. Iodine typically has an oxidation number of 1−. Explain why this is or is not true for I_2.

   _____

   _____

2. Chlorine typically has an oxidation number of 1−. Explain why this is or is not true for $NaClO_4$.

   _____

   _____

Reduction of Manganese

Potassium permanganate, $KMnO_4$, is an excellent oxidizing agent. It goes through a series of color changes as it is reduced. The variety of colors it produces shows that a single element can have many oxidation states. Can you name another metal that turns more than one color when exposed to oxygen?

Materials　safety goggles
　　　　　　　lab coat or apron
　　　　　　　100 mL 0.00040 M $KMnO_4$
　　　　　　　25-mL graduated cylinder
　　　　　　　four 100-mL beakers
　　　　　　　6 M HCl
　　　　　　　0.1 M $NaHSO_3$
　　　　　　　8 M NaOH
　　　　　　　3 pipets

Procedure

1. Put on safety goggles and a lab coat or apron.

2. Add 20 mL of the 0.00040 M $KMnO_4$ solution to each of four small beakers. **Safety Alert: Handle glass with care. Report any broken or chipped glass to your teacher immediately. Wipe up all spills immediately. Some chemicals are toxic. Do not get chemical on your skin or in your mouth. If this happens, report it immediately.**

3. Beaker #1 is a control and will be used for a means of comparison. Add nothing more to beaker #1.

Reduction of Manganese, continued

4. Refer to the table below when filling the remaining beakers with solutions.

Beaker	Drops of HCl	Drops of NaHSO₃	Drops of NaOH	Desired Color	Product Formed
#1				purple	MnO_4^{1-}
#2				colorless	Mn^{2+}
#3				orange	MnO_2
#4				green	MnO_4^{2-}

5. Refer to the table and find the desired color for beaker #2. Count enough drops of 6 M HCl and enough drops of 0.1 M NaHSO₃ to get the desired color. Record the number of drops in the table. When the desired color is met, permanganate will be reduced to the manganese(II) ion.

6. Refer to the table and find the desired color for beaker #3. Count enough drops of 0.1 M NaHSO₃ to get the desired color. Record the number of drops in the data table. When the desired color is met, permanganate will be reduced to the manganese(IV) oxidation state.

7. Refer to the table and find the desired color for beaker #4. Count enough drops of 8 M NaOH and 0.1 M NaHSO₃ to get the desired color. Record the number of drops in your data table. When the desired color is met, manganese will be reduced to the 2⁻ state.

Cleanup/Disposal

Wash the glassware, and return all materials. Clean your work area, and wash your hands.

Reduction of Manganese, continued

Analysis

For each product below, write the correct oxidation state.

1. MnO_4^{1-} = _____

2. Mn^{2+} = _____

3. MnO_2 = _____

4. MnO_4 = _____

Conclusions

Write the answer to each question.

1. Which solution was used in all three reduction steps? _____

2. What was the purpose of hydrochloric acid? _____

   _____

3. What was the purpose of sodium hydroxide?

   _____

4. It is possible for the sodium bisulfite to act as both an
   oxidizing agent and a reducing agent. Explain how this
   might occur.

   _____

   _____

Explore Further

The tarnishing of silver is an oxidation reaction. Silver reacts
with sulfur in the air or in certain foods. Identify a food that
contains sulfur. Design an experiment using the food and silver.
Demonstrate the time it takes for silver to tarnish when different
amounts of sulfur are present.

Traffic Light Redox

This lab puts together several concepts you have learned. There are acids and bases, reductions and oxidations, excess and limiting reagents, plus color changes. Indigo carmine is used as the indicator dye. Can you propose a different dye, and predict the color changes that would occur?

Materials   safety goggles
                lab coat or apron
                250-mL Erlenmeyer flask with a stopper
                3 g dextrose
                5 g NaOH
                100-mL graduated cylinder
                distilled water
                400-mL beaker
                stirring rod
                1.0% solution indigo carmine

Procedure

1. Put on safety goggles and a lab coat or apron.

2. Measure 250 mL of distilled water into a beaker. While stirring, add 3.0 g of dextrose and 5.0 g of NaOH. The solution should appear clear. **Safety Alert: Handle glass with care. Report any broken or chipped glass to your teacher immediately. Wipe up all spills immediately.**

3. Place 50 mL of this solution into the flask.

4. Slowly, and without swirling, add 5 to 10 mL of indigo carmine to the flask. The solution should appear yellow as the indigo carmine is reduced by the dextrose (a base).

5. Stopper the flask and gently swirl. A red color is produced as the indigo carmine is oxidized by the dissolving O_2. If the red color does not appear, add a few more drops of indigo carmine.

Traffic Light Redox, continued

6. With your thumb on the stopper, give the flask a quick shake to produce the green color. This represents even further oxidation of the indicator. If the green does not appear, open the flask to let in air.

7. Let the flask sit on your lab table. The dextrose will slowly become reduced and the solution should go back to the yellow color. Repeat steps 5 and 6 again.

Cleanup/Disposal

Flush the contents of the flask down the drain. Wash the glassware, and return all materials. Clean your work area, and wash your hands.

Analysis

1. Three substances were mixed together: dextrose, NaOH, and indigo carmine. Which one is gaining electrons in step 4?

_____

2. In step 5, the indigo carmine was oxidized by dissolved oxygen. From where did the oxygen come? _____

3. In step 6, which substance is losing electrons?

_____

Conclusions

Using your observations of steps 2 through 7, explain the exchange of electrons that occurred between each chemical in these reactions. Include such words as "oxidizing agent" and "reducing agent."

_____

_____

_____

Explore Further

Does the pH of a solution change during redox? Repeat the above procedures, using a wide-range indicator paper to determine pH.

Concentration in a Redox Reaction

Use with Investigation 18, pages 716–717

The oxidation or reduction of a reactant causes its properties to change. How does this change relate to concentration? In this investigation, you will observe the reaction given by this unbalanced equation: $Fe^{3+} + I^{1-} \rightarrow Fe^{2+} + I_2$.

Materials   safety goggles   3 medium test tubes

                lab coat or apron   grease pencil

                gloves   test-tube rack

                10-mL graduated cylinder

                15 mL of 0.20 M potassium iodide (KI) solution

                8 mL of KI solution of unknown concentration in a medium test tube

                50 mL of distilled water

                stirring rod

                40 mL of 0.20 M iron(III) chloride ($FeCl_3$) solution

                50-mL beaker

Procedure

1. Put on safety goggles, gloves, and a lab coat or apron.

2. Use the grease pencil to label the test tubes 1, 2, and 3. Place the test tubes in the rack.

3. Measure 2 mL of 0.20 M KI solution in the graduated cylinder. Pour it into tube 1. Stir in 6 mL of distilled water. **Safety Alert: Handle glassware with care. Dispose of broken glass properly.**

4. Measure 4 mL of 0.20 M KI solution and pour it into tube 2. Stir in 4 mL of distilled water.

5. Measure 8 mL of 0.20 M KI solution and pour it into tube 3.

6. Rinse the graduated cylinder with distilled water.

7. Measure 10 mL of $FeCl_3$ solution and pour it into the beaker. **Safety Alert: Iron(III) chloride is a skin irritant. Handle the solution carefully.**

8. Slowly pour the 10 mL of $FeCl_3$ solution from the beaker into tube 1. Stir the mixture and record your observations.

Concentration in a Redox Reaction, continued

9. Repeat steps 7 and 8 for tubes 2 and 3 and for the solution of unknown concentration.

Cleanup/Disposal

Pour the solutions into the proper waste containers. Wash, dry, and return the equipment. Then wash your hands.

Analysis

1. How do you know that diatomic iodine, I_2, is produced in this reaction? _____

_____

2. Compare the colors of the liquids in the four tubes after adding the $FeCl_3$. _____

_____

Conclusions

1. What are the molarities of the KI solutions in tubes 1, 2, and 3?

_____

_____

2. Estimate the unknown KI molarity. Explain your answer.

_____

_____

3. Write the half-reactions for this redox reaction.

_____

_____

4. Which element is oxidized? Which is reduced?

_____

_____

Explore Further

Find the overall balanced redox equation for the reaction that occurred in this investigation. Do potassium and chlorine appear in the equation? Explain your answer.

_____

_____

_____

Electrolysis

Use with Discovery Investigation 18, pages 735–736

Electricity can be used to produce or reverse redox reactions. The nature of these reactions depends on the amount of electricity used. It also depends on the properties of the electrolyte and its concentration. What reaction will occur when electric current is passed through a given electrolyte? In this investigation, you will observe electrolysis using several electrolytes.

Materials   safety goggles
             lab coat or apron
             9-V battery
             2 wires with alligator clips on each end
             2 graphite (carbon) rods
             petri dish
             distilled water
             0.1 M copper sulfate ($CuSO_4$) solution
             0.1 M potassium iodide (KI) solution
             0.1 M sodium chloride (NaCl) solution
             0.1 M acetic acid ($HC_2H_3O_2$) solution

Procedure

1. Predict what reactions will occur during electrolysis using distilled water and using each of the four electrolyte solutions. The graphite rods are the electrodes. Write your hypotheses. Then write a procedure for testing them. Include safety alerts.

2. Have your hypotheses and procedure approved by your teacher. Then construct your testing apparatus, shown on page 736 of your textbook.

3. Put on safety goggles and a lab coat or apron.

4. Perform your investigation. Record your observations for each solution tested.

Cleanup/Disposal

Pour the $CuSO_4$ and KI solutions into proper waste containers. Pour the NaCl and $HC_2H_3O_2$ solutions down the sink with plenty of running water. Wash and return the equipment. Wash your hands.

Electrolysis, continued

Analysis

1. Did the electrolysis using distilled water produce the result you expected? Explain your answer.

_____

2. What evidence of a reaction occurred when you used the $CuSO_4$ solution as an electrolyte? When you used the KI solution? _____

3. Compare the reactions that occurred when you used the NaCl and $HC_2H_3O_2$ solutions as electrolytes.

_____

_____

Conclusions

1. Was the cathode connected to the positive or negative terminal of the battery? Explain your answer.

_____

2. For the reactions that produced bubbles at the electrodes, which gas was produced at the anode? At the cathode? Explain your answers. _____

_____

3. Which of the four electrolytes produced the slowest reaction? Explain your answer. _____

4. The reaction at the cathode was different in the $CuSO_4$ solution than in the other solutions. Use Table 18.5.1 to explain why. _____

Explore Further

Repeat the investigation using a sodium carbonate (Na_2CO_3) solution. Compare how much gas is produced at the anode and at the cathode. Explain your results.

_____

_____

_____

Express Lab 19

Use with Express Lab 19, page 748

Materials gumdrops, plastic foam balls, or a ball-and-stick model kit
toothpicks or sticks from model kit

Procedure

1. Put on safety goggles. You will model and sketch the isomers of heptane, C_7H_{16}. For each model, use 7 carbon atoms and 16 hydrogen atoms. Every carbon atom must be bonded to four atoms.

2. Isomers differ in the way they branch. Start with a chain of 7 carbon atoms. Then model as many different heptane isomers as you can using chains of 6, 5, and 4 carbon atoms. Sketch each model you make.

Analysis

1. How many isomers of heptane are there?

   _____

2. After creating the isomers in step 2, can you create any new isomers if you start with a 3-carbon chain and add branches? Explain your answer.

   _____

   _____

Making an Ester
Use with Investigation 19, pages 759–760

Esters provide the flavors and scents of many fruits and flowers. How can you make an ester? In this investigation, you will prepare an ester by combining an alcohol and an acid. Will you be able to identify the scent of the product?

Materials
safety goggles
lab coat or apron
gloves
250-mL beaker
tap water
distilled water
hot plate
test tube

10-mL graduated cylinder
3 mL of methanol
1.5 g of salicylic acid
concentrated sulfuric acid in dropper bottle
100-mL beaker
test-tube holder
stirring rod

Procedure

1. Put on safety goggles, gloves, and a lab coat or apron.

2. Create a water bath by half-filling the large beaker with tap water. Put the beaker on a hot plate. Turn on the hot plate to medium. **Safety Alert: Do not touch the beaker with bare hands after it begins to warm. Do not leave the hot plate unattended while it is on.**

3. In the test tube, mix 3 mL of methanol, 1.5 g of salicylic acid, 3 mL of distilled water, and 5 drops of sulfuric acid, in that order. **Safety Alert: Sulfuric acid is corrosive. Handle it with care.**

4. Use the test-tube holder to place the test tube in the hot water bath on the hot plate. Leave it there for 5 minutes.

5. Add about 50 mL of distilled water to the small beaker.

6. Use the test-tube holder to remove the test tube from the hot water bath. Pour the contents into the small beaker of distilled water, and stir. Turn off the hot plate.

Making an Ester, continued

7. Allow the mixture to sit for a couple of minutes. Observe the smell of the liquid by wafting its vapors toward your nose, as shown.

Cleanup/Disposal

Dispose of the beaker contents in the proper waste container. Clean the glassware and return all equipment. Wash your hands.

Analysis

1. Describe the smell of the product of the reaction.

_____

2. Sulfuric acid is not a reactant or a product of the reaction. What purpose does sulfuric acid have in this reaction?

_____

_____

Conclusions

1. The ester, methyl salicylate, is formed when methanol and salicylic acid react. What is the other product of the reaction?

_____

2. Write a word equation for the reaction that produced the ester.

_____

Explore Further

Use reference books to find the structural formulas for methanol, salicylic acid, and methyl salicylate. Using the structural formulas, write an equation for the reaction.

_____

Linking Polymers
Use with Discovery Investigation 19, pages 769–770

When monomers bond, a polymer forms. What happens when polymers link together? White glue contains polymers. In this investigation, you will use borax to link the polymer strands in white glue to each other.

Materials

safety goggles	10-mL graduated cylinder
lab coat or apron	100-mL graduated cylinder
gloves	2 tongue depressors
50 mL of white glue	distilled water
4 paper cups	grease pencil
5 g of borax	stirring rod
2 400-mL beakers	

Procedure

1. Put on safety goggles, gloves, and a lab coat or apron.

2. Read through the entire procedure. Then design a data table you can use to record your observations.

3. Make a glue solution by mixing 50 mL of white glue and 50 mL of water in a beaker. Stir well. Using the large graduated cylinder, divide the solution evenly among the four cups. Label the cups 1, 2, 3, and 4.

4. Make a borax solution in the other beaker by dissolving about 5 g of borax in 100 mL of water.

5. Write a procedure for finding the best amount of borax solution to use to link the polymers in the white glue solution. You will judge which amount is the best by how long a strand you can form when you stretch the resulting linked polymers. In your procedure, include a hypothesis and any safety alerts.

6. After your teacher approves your procedure, perform the investigation. Test the four polymer samples.

Linking Polymers, continued

Cleanup/Disposal

Dispose of your polymer samples in a proper waste container.
Clean the glassware and return all materials. Wash your hands.

Analysis

1. Which sample produced the longest string?

_____

2. What happened to the polymers in a sample if the sample did
not pull into a string after adding borax?

_____

Conclusions

1. Explain why the polymers pulled into a long string when a
certain amount of borax was added.

_____

_____

2. Explain your answer to Analysis question 2.

_____

_____

Explore Further

Research the concept of cross-linking. Write a paragraph to explain
how cross-linking relates to this investigation.

_____

_____

_____

_____

Milk Analysis

Have you ever thought of milk as a nutritious snack? Whole milk contains protein, carbohydrates, fat, water, vitamins, and minerals. Which biological molecule is found in the greatest percentage in whole milk? In this investigation, you will find out.

Materials   safety goggles   pipet
                   lab coat or apron   stirring rod
                   25-mL graduated cylinder   pipestem triangle
                   20 mL nonfat milk   funnel
                   100-mL beaker   cheesecloth
                   250-mL beaker   distilled water
                   400-mL beaker   spatula or wood splint
                   electronic balance   dehydrating oven
                   concentrated acetic acid   large evaporating dish

Procedure

1. Put on safety goggles and a lab coat or apron.

2. Place the graduated cylinder on the electronic balance and tare out its mass. Place the cylinder on the balance. Press the tare button. The display should read 0.00. The balance will ignore the mass of the graduated cylinder. Do not remove the cylinder. Measure out 15.0 mL of nonfat milk in the graduated cylinder. Record its mass in the data chart. **Safety Alert: Handle glass with care. Report any broken or chipped glass to your teacher immediately. Wipe up all spills immediately. Digital balances are extremely accurate and sensitive measuring devices. Do not press on the pan. Avoid spilling on it.**

	15.0 mL of Milk	Cheesecloth	Dried Milk Curds	5.0 mL of Milk	Evaporating Dish	Milk Solids after Evaporation	Evaporated Water
mass (g)							

Milk Analysis, continued

3. Pour the milk into a small beaker. Add 30 drops of concentrated acetic acid. Stir gently. Allow the beaker to sit for 5 minutes.

4. Place a pipestem triangle on a second, medium-sized beaker. Place a funnel in the triangle.

5. Measure and record the mass of your cheesecloth. Line the funnel with the cheesecloth.

6. Pour the coagulated milk into the funnel. Add 2 mL of distilled water to the empty beaker and swirl. Pour this into the funnel. Use a spatula or wooden splint to scrape out any remaining curds.

7. Place cheesecloth with curds on a watch glass and place the watch glass in an oven to dry. Measure and record the mass of the dried curds on the cheesecloth. Dispose of the curds and cheesecloth in the proper waste container.

8. Place the cleaned graduated cylinder on the electronic balance again and tare out its mass. Measure and record the mass of 5.0 mL of nonfat milk in the graduated cylinder.

9. Measure and record the mass of the large evaporating dish.

10. Fill a large beaker half full with tap water. Place on the hot plate. Balance the evaporating dish atop the beaker. Pour in the milk. Heat the milk until all water has evaporated. **Safety Alert: Use care around hot objects. Report any burns immediately.**

11. Measure and record the mass of the milk solids in the evaporating dish. Determine the mass of water that evaporated and record it in your data chart.

Cleanup/Disposal

Wash the glassware, and return all materials. Clean your work area, and wash your hands.

Milk Analysis, continued

Analysis

1. Calculate the percent of protein in your milk sample.

_____

2. Calculate the percent of water in your milk sample.

_____

3. Calculate the percent of carbohydrates in milk.

_____

Conclusions

1. How might the presence of milk fat change your percentages?

_____

2. Acetic acid acted as a catalyst. How would diluting this enzyme affect its ability to form curds?

_____

Explore Further

Investigate the making of cheese. How is the investigation above similar to the cheese-making process? If you wanted to make cheese at home, what steps would you have to add to this investigation?

_____

_____

_____

_____

Making Paint

Most paints consist of colored pigments combined with a binder
that keeps the paint soft. Some commercially made waterproof
artist's paints use the same technique in this investigation. The
binder for the paints in this investigation will be made from
casein, a milk protein. Color is an important aspect of paint.
What substances do you think will be used as pigments in this
investigation?

Materials safety goggles   pipestem triangle
              lab coat or apron   funnel
              skim milk   cheesecloth
              400-mL beaker   mortar and pestle
              250-mL beaker   heavy paper
              hot plate   paintbrushes (or stir rods,
              10-mL graduated cylinder   wood splints, cotton swabs, etc.)
              concentrated acetic acid pigments
              stirring rod   Making Pigments Chart

Procedure

1. Put on safety goggles and a lab coat or apron.

2. Collect 200 mL of skim milk in a beaker. The amount does not
   need to be exact. **Safety Alert: Handle glass with care. Report
   any broken or chipped glass to your teacher immediately.
   Wipe up all spills immediately.**

3. Gently heat the milk on a hot plate until it is very hot but not
   boiling. Remove the hot beaker and place it on your lab table.
   **Safety Alert: Use care around hot objects. Report any burns
   immediately.**

4. Measure 10 mL of concentrated acetic acid into a graduated
   cylinder. Slowly, while stirring, add the acetic acid to your hot
   milk. Let the mixture sit for 5 minutes.

Making Paint, continued

5. Using a pipestem triangle and funnel, filter the coagulated milk through cheesecloth. Discard the liquid into the appropriate waste container. Rinse the curds with distilled water. Gently squeeze out any remaining liquid.

6. Crumble the casein into small pieces on a watch glass. Place the watch glass in the oven and allow the casein to dry. After drying, grind it into a powder with a mortar and pestle.

7. Place a small amount of the powdered casein (enough to cover a penny) into a small beaker. Add just enough distilled water to make a thick paste. Stir until smooth.

8. Look at the Making Pigments Chart on page 3 and select a color to make. Mix up the pigment as instructed in the chart. Add the pigment to your casein paste and stir until the desired color is obtained.

9. Get a piece of heavy paper from your teacher. Paint a picture using brushes, stirring rods, wood splints, cotton swabs, etc.

Cleanup/Disposal

Wash the glassware, and return all materials. Clean your work area, and wash your hands.

Analysis

1. How is the protein casein separated from the milk chemically?

_____

2. List three properties that paints need to have in order to be useful. _____

_____

Conclusions

1. Why was it necessary to boil the milk first? _____

2. Casein is also used to make other products. Observe some of the qualities of casein-based paints. List other items you think could be made from a casein-based substance.

_____

Making Paint, continued

Explore Further

Research the substance "latex." Discuss the similarities and differences when compared to the casein-based paint you made.

Making Pigments Chart

COLOR	DIRECTIONS
black	Use charcoal mixed directly with the casein paste
navy blue	Place 0.2 g of $NH_4Fe(SO_4)_2 \cdot 3H_2O$ in a test tube. Fill $\frac{1}{2}$ full with warm water. Stopper and shake until dissolved. Add 0.2 g of $K_4Fe(CN)_6$ to the tube. Stopper and shake until dissolved. Filter the solution. Discard the liquid filtrate. Mix the precipitated pigment with the casein paste.
royal blue	Place 0.2 g of $CoCl_2$ in a test tube. Fill $\frac{1}{2}$ full with warm water. Stopper and shake until dissolved. Add 2.0 mL of Na_2SiO_3 to the tube. Stopper and shake until dissolved. Filter the solution. Discard the liquid filtrate. Mix the precipitated pigment with the casein paste.
pale yellow-green to brown	Place 0.2 g of $NH_4Fe(SO_4)_2 \cdot 3H_2O$ in a test tube. Fill $\frac{1}{2}$ full with warm water. Stopper and shake until dissolved. Add 0.2 g of Na_2CO_3 to the tube. Stopper and shake until dissolved. Filter the solution. Discard the liquid filtrate. Mix the precipitated pigment with the casein paste.
gray-green	Place 0.4 g of $K_4Fe(CN)_6$ in a test tube. Fill $\frac{1}{2}$ full with warm water. Stopper and shake until dissolved. Add 0.2 g of $CoCl_2$ to the tube. Stopper and shake until dissolved. Avoid touching the $CoCl_2$. Filter the solution. Discard the liquid filtrate. Mix the precipitated pigment with the casein paste.
lavender	Place 0.2 g of $CoCl_2$ in a test tube. Fill $\frac{1}{2}$ full with warm water. Stopper and shake until dissolved. Add 0.2 g of Na_2CO_3 to the tube. Stopper and shake until dissolved. Filter the solution. Discard the liquid filtrate. Mix the precipitated pigment with the casein paste.
orange	Place 0.2 g of $NH_4Fe(SO_4)_2 \cdot 3H_2O$ in a test tube. Fill $\frac{1}{2}$ full with warm water. Stopper and shake until dissolved. Add 1.0 mL of Na_2SiO_3 to the tube. Stopper and shake until dissolved. Filter the solution. Discard the liquid filtrate. Mix the precipitated pigment with the casein paste.
white	Place 0.3 g of $CaCl_2$ in a test tube. Fill $\frac{1}{2}$ full with warm water. Stopper and shake until dissolved. Add 0.3 g of Na_2CO_3 to the tube. Stopper and shake until dissolved. Filter the solution. Discard the liquid filtrate. Mix the precipitated pigment with the casein paste.